WORLD SERIES
100TH ANNIVERSARY
2003

An American
CLASSIC
THE WORLD SERIES AT 100

WORLD CHAMPIONSHIP TROPHY

WRITTEN AND EDITED BY
Ken Leiker
ART DIRECTION BY
Nick De Carlo

Rare Air Media

Designed and Produced by

RARE AIR BOOKS
A DIVISION OF RARE AIR MEDIA

AN AMERICAN CLASSIC
THE WORLD SERIES AT 100

For information contact Rare Air Media, 2835 N. Sheffield, Suite 215, Chicago, Illinois 60657
www.rareairmedia.com

A Ballantine Book
The Random House Publishing Group

Photography except as noted below © Corbis-Bettman Archives

Tom G. Lynn, *Time Life Pictures, Getty Images*	79
MLB photos	1, 6-11, 26, 27, 55-56, 60-61
National Baseball Hall of Fame Library, Cooperstown, NY	36, 37, 87
Jeffrey Phelps, *Time Life Pictures, Getty Images*	79
Rich Pilling, *MLB photos*	81
Rick Stewart, *Getty Images*	52, 53, 96
Ron Vesely, *MLB photos*	23
Michael Zagaris, *MLB photos*	97

www.ballantinebooks.com

Library of Congress Cataloging-in-Publication Data can be obtained from the publisher upon request.

ISBN 0-345-46091-X

Manufactured in the United States of America

First Edition: December 2003

2 4 6 8 10 9 7 5 3 1

ACKNOWLEDGMENTS

At Rare Air Media, making a book is not a labor, but rather a celebration of the creative process. We were reminded of that again as this book took on the substance and style that comes from people who constantly challenge their imaginations and refuse to wear watches. A model that demands both unequaled editorial integrity and production quality was set in place by Mark Vancil, who continues to lead the company to greater thresholds and blaze new trails in book publishing.

Rare Air books are recognized worldwide for striking design and visual impact, and for that we are grateful to Nick De Carlo and John Vieceli, who again showed an endless capacity for creating pages that reverberate with energy and emotion.

The pictures in this book span a century. Locating and selecting them was a daunting task that we could not have accomplished without the assistance of our imagery experts at Corbis-Bettman (Bill O'Connor and Michael Bacino), Major League Baseball (Paul Cunningham), the National Baseball Hall of Fame (Bill Burdick) and Getty Images (Howie Burke).

On a personal level, my lineup includes all superstars. Thank you, Cherié, James, Nicole and Courtney. And a special citation for Taylor, the youngest, who has discovered the joy of baseball, even though she roots for the Cubs.

— Ken Leiker

★★ SPECIAL THANKS ★★

At Major League Baseball, Don Hintze remains a committed partner and the very best at what he does in the business of professional sports. His dedication, character and compassion is unique and makes an otherwise challenging process effortless. All of this work came together thanks to the commitment and support of everyone at Ballantine Books, specifically Gina Centrello, Anthony Ziccardi, Bill Takes, Zach Schisgal, Patricia Nicolescu and Kathy Rosenbloom.

— Mark Vancil

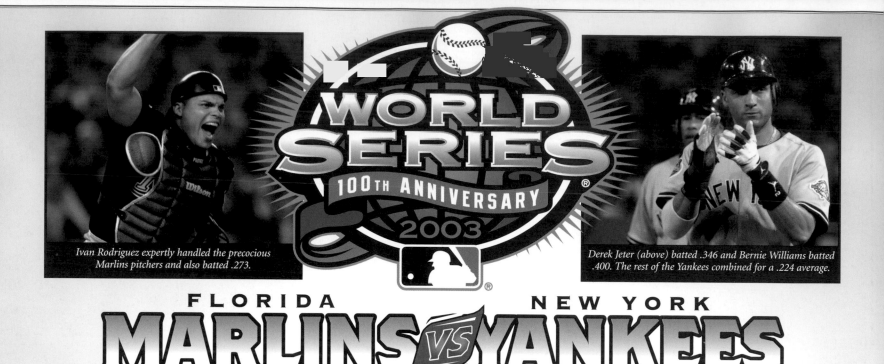

WORLD SERIES
100TH ANNIVERSARY
2003

Ivan Rodriguez expertly handled the precocious Marlins pitchers and also batted .273.

Derek Jeter (above) batted .346 and Bernie Williams batted .400. The rest of the Yankees combined for a .224 average.

FLORIDA
NEW YORK
MARLINS vs YANKEES

The 99th World Series began with much of the baseball-conscious world still drunk from anticipation of a Chicago Cubs–Boston Red Sox matchup. The Cubs have not won the world championship since 1908 and the Red Sox since 1918 — one under the curse of a long-dead billy goat owner, the other doomed since trading off Babe Ruth — but each stirred the imagination in the league championship series before bowing out. Left were the New York Yankees and the Florida Marlins, baseball aristocracy versus a National League upstart — the second one in three years. In 2001 the four-year-old Arizona Diamondbacks stunned the Yankees in the World Series. Two years later, it was the 11-year-old Marlins who showed up.

Jack McKeon got the first World Series ride of his 54-year professional career.

ROGER CLEMENS	IP	H	R	ER	BB	SO	
GAME 4	7	8	3	3	0	5	

THIS WAS TO BE A PASSING OF THE TORCH BETWEEN
TWO HARD-THROWING, TALL TEXANS
WHO HAD ATTENDED HIGH SCHOOLS 25 MILES AND 18 YEARS APART.

JOSH BECKETT	IP	H	R	ER	BB	SO	
GAME 3	$7^{1/3}$	3	2	2	3	10	
GAME 6	9	5	0	0	2	9	

It is never a surprise when the Yankees qualify for the World Series. This was their 39th, their sixth since 1996, and they had won 26, almost three times as many as any other team. The Marlins won the World Series in 1997, when just five years old, but mostly they had lived a precarious existence in south Florida, unable to attract a large and enduring ticket-buying fan base. The Marlins began 2003 full of youthful exuberance and promise, but soon fell into last place in their division. They fired their manager in May and replaced him with 72-year-old Jack McKeon, who had last been seen in the major leagues three years earlier, but

Maynard G. Krebs goatee, beat the Cubs with a two-hit shutout and three days later sealed their fate with four innings of splendid relief pitching. Beckett clearly rose above the fray, and he sent the Marlins' hopes soaring because he would be the starter in two games against the Yankees.

This was to be a passing of the torch between two hard-throwing, tall Texans who had attended high schools 25 miles and 18 years apart. Roger Clemens of the Yankees was finishing up a brilliant 20-year major league career; Beckett, in his third season, was coming into his own. The teams split the first two games in

RIGHT: Aaron Boone (19) saluted Hideki Matsui after Matsui's three-run home run put the Yankees in command of Game 2.

BELOW: Juan Pierre's speed on the bases was a constant annoyance to the Yankees.

ABOVE: Alex Gonzalez eluded Jorge Posada's tag and scored in the fifth inning of Game 6 — the only run the Marlins would need.

LEFT: Derek Jeter's three hits in Game 3 were the only ones against Josh Beckett.

insisted that he had not retired — "I was between jobs," he said. The callow Marlins took to their sage mentor, climbed out of their hole, achieved the best record in the major leagues from May 23 onward, and qualified for the playoffs as a wildcard team with the second winning record in their 11 seasons.

The Marlins needed to win the final three games against the Cubs to get to the World Series. As they pulled that off, it became apparent that they had in their midst the singular element that has defined many Series champions: a dominant and supremely confident pitcher. Josh Beckett, a 23-year-old righthander with a

Yankee Stadium, then the Series moved to Florida. Beckett started Game 3 and had given up only three hits — all by Derek Jeter — and struck out 10 when he left in the eighth inning with the score tied 1-1 and Jeter on base. But the Florida bullpen failed, and Beckett was charged with a 6-1 loss.

A day later, Clemens took the mound for the final time. He gave up three runs in the first inning, but then shut out the Marlins for the next six. His final pitch was a third strike past Luis Castillo to end the seventh inning. Clemens

Ivan Rodriguez celebrated the Marlins' second world championship in the team's 11-year history — as many as the Cubs, Indians and White Sox each have won since 1903.

tracking the world series

	series eligible	total series	total won	last series	last won
New York Yankees	1903-now	39	26	2003	2000
St. Louis Cardinals	1903-now	15	9	1987	1982
New York Giants	1903-1957	14	5	1954	1954
Chicago Cubs	1903-now	10	2	1945	1908
Boston Red Sox	1903-now	9	5	1986	1918
Cincinnati Reds	1903-now	9	5	1990	1990
Los Angeles Dodgers	1958-now	9	5	1988	1988
Detroit Tigers	1903-now	9	4	1984	1984
Brooklyn Dodgers	1903-1957	9	1	1956	1955
Philadelphia Athletics	1903-1954	8	5	1931	1930
Pittsburgh Pirates	1903-now	7	5	1979	1979
Oakland Athletics	1968-now	6	4	1990	1989
Baltimore Orioles	1954-now	6	3	1983	1983
Cleveland Indians	1903-now	5	2	1997	1948
Atlanta Braves	1966-now	5	1	1999	1995
Philadelphia Phillies	1903-now	5	1	1993	1980
Chicago White Sox	1903-now	4	2	1959	1917
New York Mets	1962-now	4	2	2000	1986
Minnesota Twins	1961-now	3	2	1991	1991
Washington Senators	1903-1960	3	1	1933	1924
San Francisco Giants	1958-now	3	0	2002	—
Florida Marlins	1993-now	2	2	2003	2003
Toronto Blue Jays	1977-now	2	2	1993	1993
Boston Braves	1903-1952	2	1	1948	1914
Milwaukee Braves	1953-1965	2	1	1958	1957
Kansas City Royals	1969-now	2	1	1985	1985
San Diego Padres	1969-now	2	0	1998	1998
Anaheim Angels	1961-now	1	1	2002	2002
Arizona Diamondbacks	1998-now	1	1	2001	2001
Milwaukee Brewers	1970-now	1	0	1982	1982
St. Louis Browns	1903-1953	1	0	1944	1944

These active teams have never played in the World Series:

Colorado Rockies (1993-now); Houston Astros (1962-now); Montreal Expos (1969-now); Seattle Mariners (1977-now); Tampa Bay Devil Rays (1998-now); Texas Rangers (1972-now)

These defunct teams never played in the World Series:

Kansas City Athletics (1955-1967); Seattle Pilots (1969); Washington Senators (1961-1971)

Ivan Rodriguez celebrated the Marlins' second world championship in the team's 11-year history — as many as the Cubs, Indians and White Sox each have won since 1903.

Brad Penny won Game 1 and Game 5, giving up four runs in 12 ¹/₃ innings.

Carl Pavano pitched splendidly in two games, yielding one run in nine innings.

Yankees starters David Wells, Andy Pettitte and Mike Mussina combined for a 2-2 record, despite yielding only five earned runs in 30 ²/₃ innings, a 1.47 ERA.

pumped his right fist, and the huge crowd broke into a resounding ovation. The pitcher responded with several cap-tipping gestures. The Yankees tied the score with two runs in the ninth inning, but Florida won in the 12th on Alex Gonzalez's home run. The Marlins also won Game 5, 6-2, behind the solid pitching of Brad Penny, who had also gained the victory in Game 1.

Now it was back to New York, where the Yankees had to win twice. Beckett was McKeon's choice to pitch Game 6, despite the fact that the young pitcher had never started in his professional career a game on three days' rest. McKeon retorted that Beckett had never pitched a complete game either, until his shutout of the Cubs 13 days earlier. Unfazed by the historical trappings and the hostile crowd all around him, Beckett never faltered. He gave up only five hits, struck out nine and was so thoroughly dominant that TV announcer Joe Buck at one point noted that although the Marlins had only a 2-0 lead, "it doesn't *feel* that close." When that became the final score, the Marlins had much to celebrate. They had become the second team to win the Series after being 10 games below .500 during the season — the 1914 Boston Braves were the other. They had given their grizzled manager, in his 54th professional season, his first World Series ring. They had humbled a team whose payroll was more than three times higher than theirs, proving that money isn't always the mark of a champion, even in the modern era of baseball.

The Marlins had done it the old-fashioned way, in the tradition started by the Boston Pilgrims in the first World Series in 1903. Bill Dineen and Cy Young pitched all but two innings for the Pilgrims and combined for five victories — it was a best-of-nine series — and a 1.96 ERA. One hundred years later, Beckett, Penny and Carl Pavano pitched 37 $^2/_3$ of Florida's 56 innings and combined for three victories and a 1.43 ERA. As in life, the more things change in baseball, the more they remain the same.

TABLE OF ★ CONTENTS

★ ★ ★ ★ ★ ★ ★ ★ ★ ★ ★ ★ ★ ★ ★ ★ ★

∞ 1924 ∞
WASHINGTON SENATORS DEFEATED NEW YORK GIANTS

∞ 2001 ∞
ARIZONA DIAMONDBACKS DEFEATED NEW YORK YANKEES

∞ 1947 ∞
NEW YORK YANKEES DEFEATED BROOKLYN DODGERS

∞ 1991 ∞
MINNESOTA TWINS DEFEATED ATLANTA BRAVES

∞ 1955 ∞
BROOKLYN DODGERS DEFEATED NEW YORK YANKEES

∞ 1986 ∞
NEW YORK METS DEFEATED BOSTON RED SOX

∞ 1960 ∞
PITTSBURGH PIRATES DEFEATED NEW YORK YANKEES

∞ 1975 ∞
CINCINNATI REDS DEFEATED BOSTON RED SOX

∞ 1962 ∞
NEW YORK YANKEES DEFEATED SAN FRANCISCO GIANTS

★ ★ ★ ★ ★ ★ ★ ★ ★ ★ ★ ★ ★ ★ ★ ★ ★

AN AMERICAN CLASSIC

GREAT SERIES

THE WORLD SERIES AT 100

The Giants' George Kelly crossed home plate after hitting a home run in Game 1. The catcher was Muddy Ruel.

As the 1924 baseball season drew to a close, the Washington Senators were atop the standings for the first time. This was high achievement for the U.S. capital, which had, sadly, come to exemplify this slogan: "Washington — first in war, first in peace, last in the American League." The Senators, despite hitting only 22 home runs — 24 fewer than Babe Ruth — finished two games ahead of the New York Yankees, who had Ruth and every other significant player who had helped them win the previous three pennants. Led by their 27-year-old manager, Bucky Harris, the "Boy Wonder," the Senators relied on "small ball" and the pitching of Walter Johnson, the "Big Train." Johnson had a 23-7 record, 2.72 ERA and 158 strikeouts, all league-leading totals.

Unlike Washington, the National League champion New York Giants were quite familiar with the October stage. John McGraw's mighty team was in the World Series for the fourth straight season and the eighth time in 14 years.

The Giants were favored, but public sentiment lay with the Senators, largely because the 36-year-old Johnson, arguably the greatest pitcher of all time, in his 18th season, finally had made it to the Series. Johnson, though, would lose both of his starts, 4-3 in 12 innings in Game 1 (despite striking out 12 batters), and 6-2 in Game 5. The Giants bashed Johnson for 13 hits in Game 5, including four by 18-year-old third baseman Freddie Lindstrom, as they took a three-games-to-two Series lead. Harris, the Senators' second baseman as well as their manager, was the hero in Game 6, hitting a two-run single that held up for a 2-1 victory, thanks to the pitching of Tom Zachary.

Now it was down to the seventh game, and the favored Giants were quite familiar with playing when a championship was on the line. Yet the Giants would make three errors that afternoon in Washington's Griffith Stadium and pay for them dearly. New York's 3-1 lead disappeared in the bottom of the eighth inning when the Senators loaded the bases, then scored two runs when Harris' grounder toward third base suddenly hopped and skipped over Lindstrom's head. The Senators then gave the ball to Johnson, whose resolve after two poor outings shone brilliantly. Johnson shut out the Giants for four innings. In the Senators' 12th, Giants catcher Hank Gowdy, attempting to catch Muddy Ruel's foul pop, tripped over his mask, and dropped the ball. Ruel then laced a double, and the next batter reached on an error. That brought Earl McNeely to the plate. He sent a grounder toward Lindstrom at third. The ball seemed to retrace its path of four innings earlier, taking a hop and jumping over Lindstrom's shoulder. Ruel scored, and Washington had a World Series trophy, the only one it would earn through 1972, the final season the U.S. capital had a major league team. The loss was a particularly bitter pill for the fabled McGraw, who would continue to manage the Giants until 1932 but never again make it to the Series.

The morning after the Series, Harold K. Philips of the *Washington Star* reported on a city basking in the light of baseball glory:

"Hour after hour throbbing thousands marched and rode up and down Pennsylvania Avenue; and that old thoroughfare, long accustomed to the tinseled dignity of military panoply, laughed and rocked to sounds and noises that were as strange as they were joyous to its ears. Restraint was left at home, and it was the happiest-go-luckiest mob that ever howled itself ragged."

Senators owner Clark Griffith stood on the top step of the dugout and struck a defiant pose before Game 1.

2001 | GREAT SERIES

ARIZONA DIAMONDBACKS
❧ DEFEATED ❧
NEW YORK YANKEES

Derek Jeter watched disconsolately as the Diamondbacks and their fans celebrated.

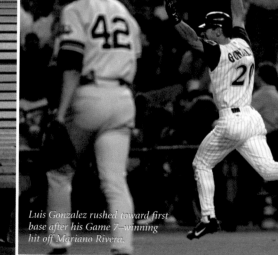

Luis Gonzalez rushed toward first base after his Game 7–winning hit off Mariano Rivera.

When the New York Yankees won the World Series for the first time in 1923, Arizona was just an 11-year-old state, the youngest of the 48. Indians still roamed the Arizona landscape — no relation to those in Cleveland. It would be 75 years later that Major League Baseball would determine Arizona was grown up enough to have a team of its own. The Arizona Diamondbacks opened play in the National League in 1998 in their sparkling new digs in Phoenix, Bank One Ballpark, and — almost as fast as a Randy Johnson fastball — the team advanced to baseball's grandest stage. The Diamondbacks arrived at the 2001 World Series with a decidedly slimmer portfolio than their

ever was the manner in which three of the games were decided. In Game 4, the Diamondbacks had a 3-1 lead with two outs in the bottom of the ninth inning, and their star relief pitcher, Byung-Hyun Kim, on the mound. Kim gave up a two-run homer to Tino Martinez that tied the score, and the Yankees won 4-3 in the 10th inning when Derek Jeter hit a home run off Kim. A day later, the Yankees struck in an almost identical fashion. Trailing 2-0 with two outs in the ninth and a runner on base, they tied the score when Scott Brosius slammed a pitch from Kim over the left-field fence. Alfonso Soriano's single in the bottom of the 12th drove home the winning run and gave the Yankees a 3-2 Series lead.

Curt Schilling

Randy Johnson

opponents, the Yankees, who by this time had taken on regal status — winners of 26 world championships, including three in a row and four in five years.

What the Diamondbacks lacked in tradition, they made up for in the game's most precious commodity: pitching. Johnson, a six-foot-ten lefthander whose crackling and bending pitches made hitters quake, and Curt Schilling, a hard-throwing righthander with the precision of a brain surgeon, formed a one-two combination that was the best in the game and among the greatest of all time. Through the season and the National League playoffs, Johnson and Schilling had a combined 48-13 record; the rest of the Diamondbacks pitchers were 51-60.

The pair would perform true to form against the Yankees, accounting for all four Arizona wins. Schilling started the first, fourth and seventh games, and was masterful in all three, giving up only four runs in 21⅓ innings. He was the winner in Game 1, turned Game 4 over to the bullpen with a 3-1 lead in the eighth inning and turned Game 7 over to the bullpen with a 2-1 deficit in the eighth inning. Johnson shut out the Yankees in Game 2, yielding three hits and striking out 11, and his Game 6 victory forced a showdown game that he also won by retiring the final four Yankees batters.

Johnson and Schilling aside, what made this one of the most gripping Series

Back in Arizona for the final two games, the Diamondbacks bludgeoned the Yankees 15-2 in Game 6. Now it was Schilling versus Roger Clemens, and the two splendid pitchers poured their souls into every pitch. Clemens had given up one run and struck out 10, leaving in the seventh with the score tied 1-1. Schilling left in the eighth, trailing 2-1 after giving up a home run to Soriano. Arizona manager Bob Brenly gave the ball first to Miguel Batista, the Game 5 starter, and then to Johnson.

Finally it was the bottom of the ninth inning. Arizona was up against Mariano Rivera, who had a career 0.70 ERA in postseason play and had not failed in 23 successive postseason save opportunities dating to 1998. A single, an error and a double tied the score. Rivera then hit a batter, which loaded the bases and brought to the plate Luis Gonzalez, who had hit 57 home runs during the season. Despite a mighty swing, Gonzalez made sickly contact, looping the ball just beyond the shortstop Jeter, who, like the rest of the infielders, had drawn in closer to be in position to make a play at home plate. Gonzalez's hit scored the winning run —the fourth one-run game of the Series — and put the world championship trophy in the hands of the Diamondbacks. It was the quickest ascent ever from franchise birth to World Series champion.

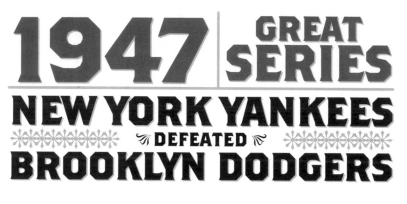

1947 | GREAT SERIES

NEW YORK YANKEES
❧ DEFEATED ❧
BROOKLYN DODGERS

This was the second "Subway Series" between the Yankees and the Brooklyn Dodgers. The Dodgers had a 28-year-old rookie first baseman, Jackie Robinson, who that year had become the first African-American to play in the big leagues. Each side had promising youngsters — Gil Hodges and Duke Snider on the Dodgers, and Yogi Berra on the Yankees — who were about to win their way into the lineup, stay there until the early 1960s and become beloved players in team history. But Hodges batted only once in the Series, Snider didn't appear at all and Berra was so deficient behind the plate that Connie Mack, sage of the Philadelphia Athletics, was moved to comment, "Never in a World Series have I seen such awful catching." Neither Robinson nor the great Joe

Jackie Robinson upended Phil Rizzuto, but Rizzuto was able to throw to first and complete a double play in Game 6. Snuffy Stirnweiss watched.

Female fans declared their allegiance before Game 1. Bill Bevens delivered a pitch in Game 4; he had a no-hitter until two outs in the ninth inning. Phil Rizzuto (10) and George McQuinn scored for the Yankees in the fifth inning of Game 1. Catcher Bruce Edwards and pitcher Ralph Branca waited for a throw to the plate.

DiMaggio performed as well as Yankees left fielder Johnny Lindell, a converted pitcher, who batted .500 and drove in seven runs. Three obscure players — Al Gionfriddo and Cookie Lavagetto of the Dodgers, and Bill Bevens of the Yankees — became instant celebrities, then faded right back into oblivion and never again played in the major leagues.

It was the first World Series to be shown on TV, and the estimated 3.9 million fans who tuned in over the seven days became television's first mass audience. The first three games produced little excitement, although Brooklyn almost squandered a 6-0 lead in Game 3 before finally prevailing 9-8. The Dodgers were confident they could tie the Series the following day, mainly because Bevens, 7-13 that season, was pitching for the Yankees. The 30-year-old Bevens was a big, husky guy who threw fairly hard but often had control problems. That would be the case in Game 4 — Bevens walked 10, a Series record — yet inning by inning he frustrated the Dodgers. Finally, it was the bottom of the ninth, and Bevens had a 2-1 lead and a no-hitter. He got two outs, but there were runners at first and second when the 34-year-old Lavagetto, coming to the plate as a pinch-hitter, sent a drive to right field that bounced off the wall. Both runners scored, and the stunned Bevens not only had lost his no-hitter, but also was the losing pitcher by a 3-2 score.

The Yankees won Game 5, and the Dodgers held an 8-5 lead in Game 6 when DiMaggio strode to the plate in the bottom of the sixth inning with two runners on base. His drive to deep left-center would have driven in two runs, except that Gionfriddo, in the game as a defensive replacement, sprinted far from where he had been positioned in left field and, with a desperate leap, made a lunging catch that is widely regarded as one of the most spectacular feats in Series history.

A day later, a champion needed to be determined. The Yankees took a 3-2 lead in the bottom of the fourth, then placed their trust in Joe Page, a left-handed reliever who had won 14 games and saved 17 that season. Page had once been best known for putting a bear's carcass on an outhouse toilet seat, then sending in unsuspecting folks, among them teammate Snuffy Stirnweiss, who was so startled when he encountered the dead beast that he thought he was having a heart attack. Page had been a heavy drinker, and his life had been a mess until DiMaggio befriended the pitcher and took him in as his road roommate. After DiMaggio married Marilyn Monroe, he was asked about living with the famed actress. DiMaggio grinned and said, "It's got to be better than rooming with Joe Page."

By 1947, Page was fulfilling his considerable promise. He was at his best for the final five innings of Game 7, shutting out the Dodgers on one hit as the Yankees completed a 5-2 victory for the first of six world championships over the next seven years.

1991 | GREAT SERIES

MINNESOTA TWINS
✳✳✳ DEFEATED ✳✳✳
ATLANTA BRAVES

Game 7 of the 1991 World Series *was about to begin. Lonnie Smith, leadoff hitter for the Atlanta Braves, offered his right hand and a friendly smile to Minnesota Twins catcher Brian Harper, who did likewise. The men didn't speak; words weren't necessary. Both realized they had been on an incredible and breathtaking ride over the previous eight days; whatever happened during the next few hours could not lessen the thrill of the experience. A score would determine a winner and a loser, but mere numerals weren't going to squash the pride and satisfaction of a job well done for Smith and Harper, and all the other Braves and Twins.*

Umpire Drew Coble signaled that the Braves' David Justice was safe at the plate in the bottom of the 12th inning of Game 3. Catcher Brian Harper was late with the tag.

Kirby Puckett circled the bases triumphantly after his 11th-inning home run in Game 6 beat the Braves.

Many claim it was the best job ever done by both sides in a World Series, and there is plenty of supporting evidence. Both teams had come from the abyss, finishing first a year after finishing last. Five of the games were decided by one run; three went into extra innings; four were won on the final play. Incredibly, Game 7 combined all three of those elements, as Jack Morris shut out the Braves for 10 innings and the Twins won 1-0 on pinch-hitter Gene Larkin's single that scored Dan Gladden in the bottom of the 10th. Larkin was one of many on both sides who emerged from obscurity for a brief encounter with fame. Greg Gagne and Scott Leius of the Twins, and Mark Lemke, Jerry Willard and Smith of the Braves, all had hits that dramatically affected games.

But when a guiding light is needed, look for the biggest star. There was no bigger star on either side in this Series than Kirby Puckett, the Twins center fielder whose roly-poly physique, unflagging hustle and effervescent personality never failed to warm a fan's ballpark experience, even in the cold, drab Metrodome, home of the Twins.

Puckett had only three hits in 18 at-bats in the first five games, each won by the home team, which meant the Braves had a 3-2 edge. The Series returned to Minneapolis for Game 6, and Puckett took it upon himself to assure that this captivating Series indeed would live another day.

In the first inning, he hit a triple that drove in a run and then scored on a single. In the third, he leaped and stretched mightily against the Plexiglas shield atop the center-field fence and snatched Ron Gant's drive before it could become a home run. In the fifth, he hit a sacrifice fly that gave the Twins a 3-2 lead. In the eighth, he singled and stole second, but was stranded there. In the 11th, he whaled into a changeup thrown by Charlie Leibrandt and socked it over the fence in left-center field to win the game and keep the Series alive — all in a night's work for the greatest and most popular player in Twins history. As Puckett chugged around the bases, buffeted by 51,155 shrieking fans, longtime Braves announcer Skip Caray dryly told his radio audience, "Same two teams here tomorrow." The exhausted Puckett would say, "I feel like I went 15 rounds with Evander Holyfield."

Game 7 would be just as tense. Both teams loaded the bases with fewer than two outs in the eighth inning, but failed to score. Smith made a baserunning gaffe that cost the Braves, and Lemke's unassisted double play ended the Twins' threat. With both teams still scoreless three innings later, Larkin's hit bounded into center field, and the Twins were the world champions for the second time in five years.

For the Twins, it was an ending. Their key players were aging, and by 1993 they were a last-place team that would have a nine-year run of losing records. For the youthful Braves, it was the beginning of an unprecedented run of first-place finishes still uninterrupted at the turn of the century. The Braves returned to the Series four times in the 1990s, but won only in 1995.

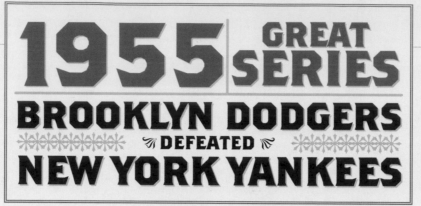

BROOKLYN DODGERS
❧ DEFEATED ❧
NEW YORK YANKEES

Brooklyn wasn't aware of it, but by the mid 1950s the Dodgers already had one foot out of town. Team owner Walter O'Malley had tried for several years to purchase Brooklyn borough land to build a park to replace dilapidated Ebbets Field, but his efforts were sabotaged by New York municipal power broker Robert Moses, whose single-minded purpose was to put a new park in Queens and bring in the Dodgers as tenants. O'Malley had no interest in such an arrangement, and so he began to survey the baseball landscape in earnest and came to the conclusion that big opportunity awaited way out west.

The Dodgers were the National League's most consistently competitive team in the 1940s and 1950s. They won the pennant in 1941, 1947, 1949, 1952 and 1953, but in each of those seasons, the Dodgers didn't prove to be even the best team in town, losing five World Series to the New York Yankees. The Dodgers won again in 1955, making short work of the pennant race by taking their first 10 games and 22 of their first 24. By the end, they were 98-55 and 13½ games in the lead. Roy Campanella, the brilliant catcher who would be paralyzed in a car wreck three years later, batted .318 with 32 home runs and was the league's Most Valuable Player. Center fielder Duke Snider had 42 homers and 136 RBIs. Don Newcombe was a 20-game winner, and three others had at least 10 victories each. Yet once again, those damn Yankees, fortified by Mickey Mantle, Yogi Berra and Whitey Ford, awaited in the Series.

The Dodgers lost the first two games in Yankee Stadium, then went home to Ebbets, where their faithful braced for what seemed to be inevitable. But Johnny Podres, a blond, blue-eyed, 22-year-old lefthander who had gone only 9-10 during the season, controlled the Yankees in Game 3 with splendid use of his changeup, a baffling pitch when the

Roy Campanella, Duke Snider and Gil Hodges carried big sticks for the Dodgers.

ABOVE: *The Dodgers and their exuberant fans dashed to thank Johnny Podres after he shut out the Yankees in Game 7.* FAR LEFT: *Clem Labine was jumping for joy after earning a save in Game 5. Roy Campanella and Gil Hodges offered congratulations. The other player is Junior Gilliam.* LEFT: *Shortstop Pee Wee Reese leaped to avoid Billy Martin and threw to first to complete a double play in Game 6.*

batter is behind in the count and has to expect a fastball. Their confidence soaring now, the Dodgers also won the next two games and took a 3-2 Series lead.

The Yankees won Game 6, and then it came down to Podres versus another lefty, Tommy Byrne, who had gone 16-5 during the season and beaten the Dodgers in Game 2. The Dodgers scored a run in the sixth inning to take a 2-0 lead, and manager Walter Alston, looking for more, sent in a pinch-hitter for second baseman Don Zimmer. When the teams changed sides, Junior Gilliam, who had been in left field, moved to second, and Sandy Amoros, a quick, lithe athlete from Havana, Cuba, went to left. In the bottom of the sixth, the first two Yankees reached base, and then Berra slashed a drive toward the left-field foul line. Amoros, who had been shaded toward center field, got on his horse and, at the last instant, made a lunging dive and caught the ball. He sprung to his feet and

whipped a throw to shortstop Pee Wee Reese, who in turn relayed to first baseman Gil Hodges to complete one of the most spectacular double plays in Series history. The Yankees went meekly after that, and Podres completed a five-hitter and a 2-0 victory.

Brooklyn erupted in unadulterated joy at a long-elusive goal achieved at last. The players went to the Hotel Bossert on Montague Street to celebrate, and soon much of the borough was there, too. Citizens actually danced in the streets, according to newspaper reports.

But the wheels of change were turning. Brooklyn's first world championship also would be its last. Los Angeles city officials had clandestinely attended the Series and were soon behind closed doors with O'Malley, plotting the team's move to California, which occurred three years later.

1986 GREAT SERIES
NEW YORK METS
❦ DEFEATED ❦
BOSTON RED SOX

Jesse Orosco shut out the Red Sox for the final two innings of Game 7. Jim Rice tried to elude the tag of Mets catcher Gary Carter.

O f all the great teams in history, few found themselves in the October soup quite as often as the 1986 New York Mets. They bowed twice to the split-fingered brilliance of the Houston Astros' Mike Scott in the National League Championship Series, but won an incredible 16-inning game that spared them from seeing Scott for a third time. Then they needed a dramatic error just to live another day in the World Series. That the Mets refused to be beaten, even when the scoreboard in their own park was flashing, *Congratulations to the Red Sox!* was the supreme testament to their greatness.

Make no mistake: This was a great Mets team. Their 108-54 record tied for the third best in the NL in the 20th century. They made mincemeat of the NL East, winning the division by 21½ games. They had Gary Carter, in his prime, behind the plate, and Darryl Strawberry, just coming into his own, in right field. Keith Hernandez and Ray Knight, steady veterans, manned the corners. Tobacco-stained Lenny Dykstra and Mookie Wilson were instigators at the top of the lineup. The Mets led the league in runs scored and batting average, and weren't far off in home runs — and the offense wasn't even the best part of the team. The pitching staff had a 3.11 ERA, better even than Houston's, which had the benefit of a park about the size of Yellowstone. The starters were Dwight "Doc" Gooden, Bob Ojeda, Sid Fernandez and Ron Darling, all in their 20s and ultra-talented. That group went 66-23, and the two closers — Roger McDowell to face right-handed hitters and Jesse Orosco to face lefties — combined for 43 saves.

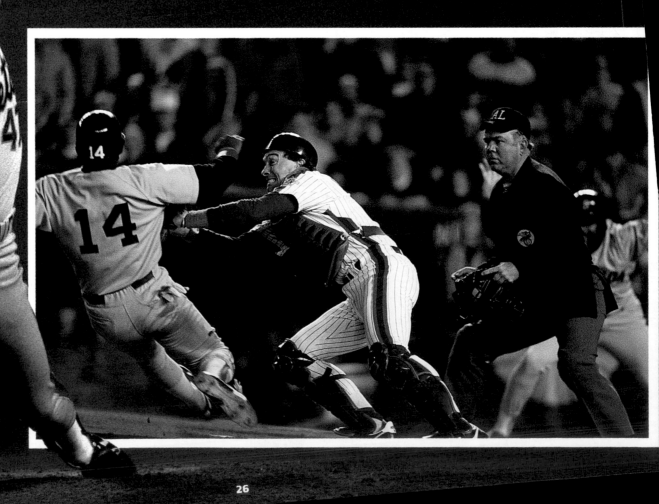

Ray Knight hustled home with the decisive run in the 10th inning of Game 6, scoring after a ball went through first baseman Bill Buckner's legs.

The Boston Red Sox had issues of their own, needing Dave Henderson's two-run homer with two outs in the ninth inning in Anaheim to stay alive in the American League Championship Series and get back to Fenway Park for the final two games. The Red Sox at the core were Bill Buckner, Don Baylor, Wade Boggs, Jim Rice and Dwight Evans, a group of veterans as tough as they come, and 23-year-old Roger Clemens, 24-4 that season, at the top of the rotation.

Five games into the Series, the Red Sox held a 3-2 advantage and headed to New York needing one victory for their first world championship in 68 years. They laid their claim in the 10th inning, scoring twice to take a 5-3 lead. The Mets came to bat and quickly made two outs. Then Carter, Kevin Mitchell and Knight all hit singles, and it was 5-4. Bob Stanley's wild pitch enabled the tying run to score.

Next was Wilson, who hit a grounder at the 36-year-old Buckner that was no different than thousands of others he had fielded over the years. But this one, instead of taking the hop that Buckner anticipated, hugged the ground and spun right through his wicket, and Knight scored the winning run.

Two days later, the Red Sox took a 3-0 lead in Game 7, but the Mets became the world champions by scoring eight runs in the final three innings for an 8-5 victory. It meant everything to the Mets and their fans, who had suffered through 90-loss seasons earlier in the decade. "When I'm on my deathbed," Hernandez declared, "my last thoughts before I die will be of this world championship."

1960 GREAT SERIES

PITTSBURGH PIRATES ✤ DEFEATED ✤ NEW YORK YANKEES

As the legend goes, the mighty 1927 New York Yankees arrived in Pittsburgh for the World Series and put on such an awesome display in batting practice that the demoralized Pirates were whipped before the first pitch of the game was thrown. The Yankees finished off the Pirates in four games, and it would be 33 years before Pittsburgh returned to the Series. The 1960 Pirates, featuring the brilliant Roberto Clemente, National League Most Valuable Player Dick Groat, Cy Young Award winner Vern Law and Dick "Dr. Strangeglove" Stuart, won 95 games, and met the Yankees once again in the Series.

The Yankees were Series regulars, having qualified for the 11th time in 14 years. No one dared say this Yankees team was comparable to the 1927 unit, but it was nonetheless very good and had a matter-of-fact confidence that bordered on arrogance. Former President Herbert Hoover and India's Prime Minister Jawaharlal Nehru were in attendance at Yankee Stadium for Game 3, and neither got as big an ovation as Yogi Berra did. Yogi didn't take that to be curious, saying in deadly earnest, "I'm a better hitter."

The greatness of this Series would be measured in awesome achievements rather than gripping, suspenseful baseball, although the latter was served up on the final day. Berra batted .318, which made him only the 12th best hitter on his team. Bobby Richardson set a Series record with 12 RBIs, and Mickey Mantle had the greatest of his 12 Series. The Yankees batted an incredible .338 as a team, easily a Series record. They won games by scores of 16-3, 10-0 and 12-0. They outscored the Pirates 55-27, and they pitched better than Pittsburgh, as evidenced by their 3.54 to 7.11 edge in ERA. The Pirates batted .256. Stuart, the slugging first baseman, failed to provide an RBI in 20 at-bats, and 18-game winner Bob Friend was 0-2 with a 13.50 ERA.

Whitey Ford delivered the first pitch of Game 3 to Bill Virdon at Yankee Stadium. The monuments dedicated to famous Yankees can be seen behind Ford in center field. He pitched a four-hitter and won 10-0.

For all the incredible things that happened during the Series, some swear the turning point actually came prior to Game 1, when Casey Stengel, the old sage of the Yankees, chose Art Ditmar to pitch first instead of Whitey Ford. Ditmar had been a 15-game winner that season and Ford had won only 12 of his 21 decisions, but Ford had a huge edge in Series experience and success. Ditmar didn't get out of the first inning, retiring only one batter, and the Yankees lost 6-4. Ditmar was ineffective again in Game 5, failing to get out of the second inning in a 5-2 loss. Ford, meanwhile, pitched two shutouts. Had the pitching rotation been set up around him, Ford might have been able to pitch a third time, in Game 7. As it was, the Yankees were on their fifth pitcher of the game, Ralph Terry, when Bill Mazeroski led off the bottom of the ninth inning with the score tied 9-9. Every baseball fan who has ever lived knows what happened next: Maz put Terry's second pitch over the ivy-covered left-field wall at Forbes Field, as dramatic a home run as any that had ever been hit or ever would be hit.

The Yankees had a huge statistical advantage, but sometimes the numbers just don't add up to what one might think they should. As Jimmy Powers of the New York *Daily News* wrote, "It was a win for the poor little guys against the big rich guys swollen with past loot and overladen with records." The blame would fall to Stengel, who had won eight world championships with the Yankees, but was nonetheless fired after the 1960 Series.

EMPTY NUMBERS

THE YANKEES STATISTICALLY DOMINATED THE PIRATES IN THE 1960 WORLD SERIES

YANKEES	BATTING	PIRATES
.338	AVERAGE	.256
55	RUNS	27
10	HOME RUNS	4
142	TOTAL BASES	83
	PITCHING	
3.54	ERA	7.11
26	STRIKEOUTS	40

Many regard the 1975 World Series between the Cincinnati Reds and the Boston Red Sox as the greatest of all time. Five of the seven games were decided by one run, two went into extra innings and one ended on a midnight home run struck by a son of New England who willed the ball fair with arms waving, a scene of high drama that has become one of baseball's signature film clips.

Baseball had lost favor in the late 1960s and early 1970s with an America torn by an unpopular war in Asia, urban racial strife and youth in revolt. Professional football's violence fed the country's psyche, which seemed too dark to appreciate and enjoy baseball's subtleties. But interest in the riveting 1975 World Series competition gained the momentum of an avalanche as the dramatic games spread out over almost two weeks. By the time Game 6 was played, after a three-day rain delay, Americans by the millions had discovered the national pastime or been lured back to it.

The Reds had won 108 games during the season, the third-best total in National League history. Their eight regular players — Johnny Bench, Tony Perez, Joe Morgan, Davey Concepcion, Pete Rose, George Foster, Cesar Geronimo and Ken Griffey, Sr. — formed one of the best lineups in history. A year later, all but Geronimo, the center fielder, made the National League All-Star team, and he batted .307 and won his third straight Gold Glove. The Red Sox, benefiting from established stars (Carl Yastrzemski, Carlton Fisk and Dwight Evans) and dynamic rookies (Fred Lynn and Jim Rice), scored 108 runs more than any other American League East team, and then upended the three-time defending world champion Oakland Athletics in the League Championship Series.

The Series began with Luis Tiant, a stocky, mustachioed Cuban with the gyrations of a conga dancer in his delivery, shutting out the Reds on five hits for a 6-0 victory. A day later, the Reds saved themselves by scoring two runs in the ninth inning and winning 3-2. Game 3 in Cincinnati was tied 5-5 after nine innings. Geronimo singled in the 10th, and then Ed Armbrister bunted. Fisk

1975 | GREAT SERIES
CINCINNATI REDS
❧ DEFEATED ❧
BOSTON RED SOX

Tony Perez connected for his second home run of Game 5, a three-run blast in the sixth inning.

burst from his position behind the plate to field the ball, but collided with Armbrister and threw wildly to second base, enabling the runners to reach second and third. The Red Sox argued that Armbrister had interfered with Fisk and should be ruled out, and that Geronimo should remain at first, but the umpires didn't agree. Morgan's fly ball deep to the outfield enabled Geronimo to score and afforded the Reds a 6-5 victory.

Tiant won again in Game 4, holding off the Reds 5-4. Perez, 0 for 15 at that point, hit two home runs and drove in four runs in Cincinnati's 6-5 victory in Game 5. The Series returned to soggy Boston, and Game 6 became one for the ages. The Reds led 6-3, but Boston tied the score in the eighth on Bernie Carbo's three-run homer, his second in the Series as a pinch-hitter, a record. The game was decided on Fisk's long drive in the 12th inning, which crashed dramatically off Fenway Park's left-field foul pole as Fisk hopped down the first-base line, frantically waving the ball fair.

Game 7 was suspenseful, as well, but given what had transpired the previous night, it was destined to be an afterthought. Boston took a 3-0 lead, but the Reds had tied the score by the seventh inning. Morgan's run-scoring shot up the middle in the ninth provided the decisive run. The Big Red Machine had its first of two consecutive world championships, the Red Sox had failed for the 57th straight year to win the Series and millions had caught baseball fever and couldn't wait until next year.

Dwight Evans was out at the plate in Game 1. Johnny Bench made the tag, and Art Frantz made the call.

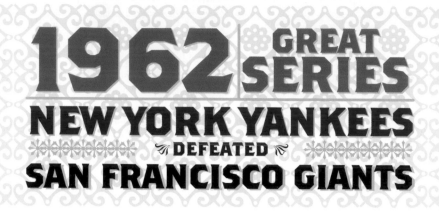

1962 | GREAT SERIES

NEW YORK YANKEES
❧ DEFEATED ❧
SAN FRANCISCO GIANTS

The 1962 season afforded Californians their first real glimpse at what New Yorkers had known since the 19th century: There's nothing in baseball quite like the intensity and downright hatred between the Giants and the Dodgers when they are in a pennant race.

Bobby Richardson slid safely into first base for an infield hit in Game 5. Willie McCovey stretched mightily for the throw.

In Game 2, Tom Haller was trapped in a rundown between third base and home plate. Third baseman Clete Boyer had the ball. First baseman Dale Long (26) waited for a throw, backed up by pitcher Ralph Terry (23). The catcher was Yogi Berra. In Game 5, Ralph Terry delivered a pitch in his complete-game victory.

Both teams had jilted New York in 1958 for San Francisco and Los Angeles respectively, but they didn't fight each other tooth and nail for first place in their new digs until four years later. The Giants were four games behind with seven games remaining but managed to pull even on the final day of the season. The rules at that time called for a three-game playoff for the pennant. Each team won a game in their home park. In the final game, the Giants stuck in the knife, staging a four-run rally in the ninth inning at Dodger Stadium for a 6-4 victory and their first trip to the World Series in eight years.

Willie Mays, Orlando Cepeda, Willie McCovey, Juan Marichal and the young Gaylord Perry — all destined for the Hall of Fame — were part of this Giants team. The offense, bolstered considerably by Mays' 49 homers and 141 RBIs, was the best in the league, and the top four starting pitchers each won at least 16 games. By comparison, the New York Yankees, American League champions for the 13th time in 16 years, were certainly formidable, but their dynastic grip on the game was loosening.

The Yankees won Game 1 with Whitey Ford earning his 10th — and final — Series victory. The teams then alternated wins for the next five games. The Yankees won both Game 3 and Game 5 by two runs. The Giants' 7-3 victory in Game 4 turned in their favor when slightly built Chuck Hiller, who had hit only three home runs in 161 games during the season, connected for the first grand slam by a National League player in Series history. Billy Pierce pitched a three-hitter for the Giants in Game 6 and won 5-2.

Game 7 in San Francisco's Candlestick Park matched Ralph Terry, a 23-game-winner for the Yankees that season, against 24-game-winner Jack Sanford. The Yankees loaded the bases in the fifth inning and scored a run as Tony Kubek hit into a double play.

The score remained 1-0 as the Giants came to bat in the bottom of the ninth. Quick little Matty Alou laid down a bunt and was safe at first — the Giants' fourth hit of the game. Terry struck out Matty's big brother, Felipe, and Chuck Hiller, but then Mays shot a double into the right-field corner. Roger Maris hustled to stop the ball before it got to the fence and returned it quickly enough to the infield that Alou had to stop at third.

Now, with two runners on base and two outs, it was up to the 24-year-old McCovey, a menacing lefthander batter who had hit a home run and a triple off Terry earlier in the Series. Yankees manager Ralph Houk had these options: 1) intentionally walk McCovey and load the bases; 2) bring in a lefthander to pitch to McCovey; 3) walk McCovey and bring in a fresh righthander to pitch to Cepeda or 4) leave it in Terry's hands, a frightening proposition for some Yankees fans; two years earlier, Terry had given up Bill Mazeroski's famous World Series–winning home run.

Houk stayed with Terry, who delivered a fastball that McCovey whaled into and slammed on a screaming line toward right field. Terry flung his glove to the ground in exasperation. But second baseman Bobby Richardson was in perfect position to snatch the ball out of the air — "certainly the hardest hit ball I've ever caught," he said — and it was over for the Giants.

★ ★ ★ ★ ★ ★ ★ ★ ★ ★ ★ ★ ★ ★ ★ ★ ★

1906
CHICAGO WHITE SOX defeated CHICAGO CUBS

1990
CINCINNATI REDS defeated OAKLAND ATHLETICS

1914
BOSTON BRAVES defeated PHILADELPHIA ATHLETICS

1988
LOS ANGELES DODGERS defeated OAKLAND ATHLETICS

1954
NEW YORK GIANTS defeated CLEVELAND INDIANS

1969
NEW YORK METS defeated BALTIMORE ORIOLES

★ ★ ★ ★ ★ ★ ★ ★ ★ ★ ★ ★ ★ ★ ★ ★ ★

AN AMERICAN CLASSIC

GREAT UPSETS

THE WORLD SERIES AT 100

1906

CHICAGO WHITE SOX
~ DEFEATED ~
CHICAGO CUBS

Third baseman Lee Tannehill was the weakest hitter among the "Hitless Wonders" regulars. He batted .183 in 116 games during the season, and he went 1 for 9 during the World Series.

Long before Major League Baseball started urging people to catch baseball fever, the city of Chicago had a raging dose. It was 1906, and both the Cubs and the White Sox finished atop their leagues — a circumstance that would not repeat itself for the remainder of the 20th century. Chicago had the World Series all to itself, and that toddlin' town was ablaze in glory. "Many of the Windy City fans collapsed completely, while others were consigned to retreats for the 'cuckoo,'" wrote MacLean Kennedy in the 1929 book The Great Teams of Baseball. *While Chicagoans were split along geographical lines in their rooting sentiment, everyone conceded that Frank Chance's Cubs were the superior team. That was an understatement.*

Shortstop George Davis missed the first three games of the World Series because of an injury, but he batted .308 in the final three games.

The 1906 Cubs set standards that have rarely (and in some cases never) been equaled. They went 116-36, a .763 winning percentage, and won the pennant by 20 games. They ranked first in the National League in batting, pitching and fielding. They outscored their opponents by an absurd margin of 705-381. The team ERA of 1.75 is the second best of all time, bettered only by the same staff a year later. Tinker to Evers to Chance, the Cubs' double-play combination, to this day rings familiar with baseball fans. Chance, the "Peerless Leader," despite his name left nothing to chance. He constantly challenged his players, even encouraging them to frequent the racetrack and poker table because betting endeavors "stirred up mental activity." Chance often played poker with a player he was considering for the Cubs to gain a feel for the man's guile and intuition.

Over on the South Side, the White Sox had needed a 19-game winning streak in August to pull themselves out of fourth place. Like the Cubs, the Sox had exceptional pitching, but their .230 batting average, .286 slugging percentage, and six home runs were pathetic marks that ranked last in the American League. Little wonder why the White Sox were referred to around town as the "Hitless Wonders."

What little chance the Sox had seemed to dissipate even more when their best player, shortstop George Davis, destined for the Hall of Fame, was unable to play in the first three games because of injury. The Sox moved third baseman Lee Tannehill to shortstop and put little-used George Rohe at third. By the time Davis was ready to play, Rohe was doing so well that he remained in the lineup and Tannehill went to the bench. By the end of the Series, Davis and Rohe had combined for a .324 batting average, 6 runs, and 10 RBIs; the rest of the Sox batted .170 with 16 runs and 9 RBIs.

It is amazing what a beam of hope can do. The Sox got two runs in Game 1 on uncharacteristic misplays by the Cubs' fine catcher, Johnny Kling, and made off with a 2-1 victory. After four games, the Sox were still in it, tied in victories, even though they had scored but six runs and batted .097. Davis delivered two hits and three RBIs in the Sox's 8-6 victory in Game 5, and he did the same thing a day later against weary Three Finger Brown, a 26-game winner for the season but now pitching for the second time in three days. The Sox finished off the Cubs 8-3, becoming perhaps the most improbable world champions in baseball history.

Jose Rijo acknowledged Reds fans at the Oakland Coliseum as he left Game 4 during the ninth inning. Soon, the Reds were celebrating their first world championship in 14 years.

1990

CINCINNATI REDS
~ DEFEATED ~
OAKLAND ATHLETICS

The Oakland Athletics dominated Major League Baseball from 1988 to 1990, winning 306 games and three American League pennants, and finishing a combined 29 games in first place. No other team had a set of sluggers the equal of Jose Canseco and Mark McGwire. No other team in history had a leadoff hitter the equal of Rickey Henderson. Dave Stewart, the A's top starter, won at least 20 games for four consecutive seasons. Bob Welch won 27 games in 1990, the highest total in 18 years. Dennis Eckersley had perhaps the greatest season ever by a relief pitcher in 1990, saving 48 games, fashioning an 0.61 ERA, and giving up only four walks while striking out 73 in 63 games.

Yet these A's were star-crossed. Heavily favored in all three World Series, they managed to win only in 1989. The talent-challenged Los Angeles Dodgers stunned the A's in five games in 1988, and the Cincinnati Reds shockingly swept Oakland in four games in 1990.

The Reds were considered a good team, but not great. They had a 91-71 record and led the National League West from start to finish, then beat the Pittsburgh Pirates in six games — four decided by one run — in the League Championship Series. None of the Reds hit as many as 25 home runs or had as many as 90 RBIs during the season, and the ace of the pitching staff, Jose Rijo, was just a 14-game winner. Three relief pitchers who called themselves the "Nasty Boys" — Rob Dibble, Randy Myers and Norm Charlton — were instrumental to the Reds' success.

The A's had won 10 consecutive postseason games, including a sweep of the San Francisco Giants in the 1989 Series, but that streak came to a thudding halt in Game 1 against the Reds. Perhaps the turning point of the entire Series came in the first inning. With two outs, Eric Davis, playing despite a sore shoulder that made it painful for him to swing a bat, drove a pitch from Stewart over the center-field fence at Cincinnati's Riverfront Stadium for a two-run home run. Davis' blast seemed to smash any air of invincibility around the A's and Stewart, who had won his previous six postseason starts. The Reds had a time of it after that, winning 7-0, with Rijo dominating the A's for seven innings.

Game 2 is regarded as one of the best in Series history. The Reds tied the score 4-4 in the eighth inning when Billy Hatcher hit a triple — his Series-record seventh straight hit — and scored on a groundout. The score remained tied until the 10th, when the Reds scored against the right-handed Eckersley with three singles, the first by Billy Bates, who had been 0 for 8 for the Reds during the season, and the last by Joe Oliver, a .179 hitter against right-handed pitchers. Four Reds relief pitchers shut out the A's for 7 1/3 innings.

The Series went to Oakland for Game 3. Chris Sabo hit two home runs for the Reds, who had an 8-2 lead after batting in the third inning, and won 8-3. It was Rijo versus Stewart again in Game 4. By the second inning, the Reds had lost both Hatcher, who suffered a hand injury when hit by a Stewart pitch, and Davis, who injured a kidney diving for a ball. The Reds fell behind 1-0 in the first, but Rijo then retired 20 consecutive batters before handing Myers the ball and a 2-1 lead with one out in the ninth. Myers got the final two outs, affording the Reds a niche in history. No team with so few victories during the season had ever won a Series in four games. The Reds did it decisively, outscoring the A's 27-8 and outhitting them 45-28.

1914

BOSTON BRAVES ~DEFEATED~ PHILADELPHIA ATHLETICS

World Series spectators jammed the roofs of row houses across the street from Philadelphia's Shibe Park.

Braves third baseman Charlie Deal.

The 1914 Boston Braves were dead last among the eight National League teams on July 4. They certainly had earned it, and the lowly franchise seemed likely to finish in last place for the fifth time in six years. The Braves were a collection of castoffs and kids, deficient in talent and experience, the vital lifelines for a successful team in any sport.

Asked for a description of his team, manager George T. Stallings sighed, and said, "One .300 hitter, the worst outfield that ever flirted with sudden death, three pitchers and a good working combination around second base." That combination was second baseman Johnny Evers, who had come from the Cubs, where he had been the keystone in the famed Tinker-to-Evers-to-Chance link, and daffy shortstop Rabbit Maranville, who was just getting started. (Maranville once said, "There is much less drinking now than there was before 1927 because I quit drinking on May 24, 1927.") At most of the other stops in the lineup, Stallings had to improvise. With nothing to lose except his job, he became the first National League manager to platoon players, resulting in 16 Braves getting at least 100 at-bats that season. As far as pitching was concerned, Stallings determined that the best strategy was to give the ball as often as possible to Dick Rudolph, Bill James and Lefty Tyler. Those three would account for 77 percent of the Braves' wins and 66 percent of the innings pitched.

Stallings' lineup machinations and ego stoking seemed to work. As the Braves gained confidence and took on a rowdy, rollicking identity, their manager implemented only one rule: "Do what you want, but don't wind up in jail, and come to play every day." The Braves began winning in mid July and quickly gained momentum and confidence. From 35-43 and last place on July 18, they went to 59-48 and first place in five weeks, an achievement that moved owner Jim Gaffney to reward the players with new caps.

The Braves then separated from the pack, winning the pennant by 10½ games. Boston won 51 of its final 67 games. The team came to be known as the "Miracle Braves," a moniker that hardly impressed Connie Mack's mighty Philadelphia Athletics, who had won three of the previous four World Series and

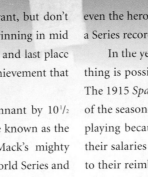

were back again. The A's had scored 134 more runs than any other American League team that season. Their famed $100,000 infield was still in place, and they had three pitchers — Chief Bender, Eddie Plank and Herb Pennock — destined for the Hall of Fame. Bender, 17-3 that season, had so little regard for the Braves that he went fishing on an off day rather than joining an expedition to scout the NL champions. "Why scout a bush league team?" he said.

Bender paid for such insolence, taking a 7-1 pounding in Game 1 in his home park, his first loss in 10 Series appearances. Game 2 was scoreless into the ninth inning, when the Braves scored on two hits and made off with a 1-0 victory. Now, the Series was going to Boston, where fervor for the Braves had grown so keen that the rival Red Sox allowed them to use two-year-old Fenway Park instead of their dilapidated digs. The A's did their damnedest in Game 3 to slow the upstarts, forging their only lead of the Series, only to be undone by a throwing error in the 12th inning and losing 5-4. A day later, Philadelphia expired meekly, 3-1. The great Macksmen scored just six runs and batted .172 in the four games.

Evers batted .438 for the Braves. He wasn't even the hero. That honor went to catcher Hank Gowdy, whose .545 average was a Series record.

In the years to come, the Braves were often held up as an example that anything is possible when an entire group plays with joy, passion and selflessness. The 1915 *Spalding Baseball Guide* had this to say: "It was hard to convince some of the seasoned baseball patrons that here was a team that actually seemed to be playing because the players liked it and were not confining their thoughts to their salaries or worrying for fear that they might work too hard in proportion to their reimbursement."

BACKGROUND: *Manager George T. Stallings sat smugly with his ace pitchers, Bill James and Dick Rudolph, who each beat Philadelphia twice.*
INSET: *The stunned A's sat disconsolately in their dugout.*

LOS ANGELES DODGERS
~ DEFEATED ~
OAKLAND ATHLETICS

1988

DAVIS
37

Mike Davis and Orel Hershiser celebrated after Davis' two-run home run in Game 5 gave the Dodgers a 4-1 lead. Mike Scioscia also offered a hand.

The 1988 Los Angeles Dodgers did not have a .300 hitter, a 30-homer man or a 100-RBI producer. Their top hitters were Kirk Gibson, who had 25 home runs and 76 RBIs, and Mike Marshall, who had 20 homers and 82 RBIs. The Dodgers had fabulous pitching, led by Orel Hershiser, but they were still considered overachievers when they won the National League West. When they beat the powerful New York Mets in the League Championship Series, it was considered amazing. When they went to the World Series, it was probably more than even their eternally optimistic manager, Tommy Lasorda, could have hoped for.

Awaiting the Dodgers were the Oakland Athletics, who had won 104 games during the season, most in the American League since the 1970 Baltimore Orioles. The A's not only had prolific sluggers Jose Canseco and Mark McGwire, who had combined for 74 homers and 223 RBIs, but also exceptional pitching, led by 21-game winner Dave Stewart and 45-saves man Dennis Eckersley.

Meanwhile, the Dodgers' Gibson was hurting, almost immobile with pain in the knees and hamstrings. Prior to Game 1, Lasorda cut short a conversation with a friend, the comedian Don Rickles, for a team meeting. "You're not going to feed them some line of bull about how they're gonna win this thing without Gibson, are you?" Rickles asked.

"Yes, I am!" roared Lasorda as he waddled off.

The Series is best remembered for Gibson limping off the bench and hitting

Hershiser gave thanks after his 6-0 shutout victory over the New York Mets in Game 7 of the National League Championship Series.

the NBC broadcast booth, Bob Costas called it probably the weakest lineup ever for a Series game. Historians thought maybe the 1906 Chicago White Sox, the "Hitless Wonders," had fielded a weaker lineup. The "Hitless Wonders" had beat the crosstown Cubs, who had won 116 games that season, the most in National League history. The Dodgers were about to fashion something just as unexpected.

The Dodgers had won the first two games in Los Angeles. Mark McGwire's ninth-inning home run had given the A's a 2-1 victory in Game 3 in Oakland. Knowing that Hershiser would pitch Game 5, the A's were under considerable pressure to win Game 4, but they committed two telling errors and lost 4-3. The kill came the following night. Hershiser pitched a four-hitter, and Hatcher and Davis each hit a two-run homer in a 5-2 triumph that made the Dodgers as unlikely world champions as any that had ever been.

a two-run home run off Eckersley with two outs in the bottom of the ninth inning of Game 1 to give the Dodgers a stunning 5-4 victory. Gibson did not play again in the Series, and Marshall's aching back had him on the bench by Game 4. So the number three hitter in the Dodgers' lineup that night was Mickey Hatcher, who had had one home run and 25 RBIs during the season, and the cleanup hitter was Michael Davis, who had batted .196 with two home runs and 17 RBIs. Danny Heep, the designated hitter, had no home runs and 11 RBIs. The entire lineup had hit 36 home runs, six fewer than Canseco had hit all by himself. Up in

Some called it a testament to clean living, for the hero was the devoutly religious Hershiser, who didn't smoke, drink or swear, and hummed Christian hymns as he worked. Orel had a 23-8 record, 2.26 ERA and a major-league record 59 consecutive scoreless innings during the season; a win, a save and a 1.09 ERA in the playoffs; and two wins and a 1.00 ERA in the Series.

It had been a grand October in Los Angeles, and the memories would be lasting. Good thing, for it was last time the Dodgers would make the Series in the 20th century.

NEW YORK GIANTS ~DEFEATED~ CLEVELAND INDIANS

1954

The Giants' Sal Maglie delivered the first pitch of the Series. The batter was Al Smith, the catcher Wes Westrum and the umpire Al Barlick.

*The New York Giants were not expected to win the National League pennant in 1954.
They had finished fifth the previous year, 35 games out of first place. Willie Mays was back from the
Korean War after missing most of the 1952 season and all of 1953, but his return to the Giants
lineup wasn't enough to convince most observers that the team would be better than the
Brooklyn Dodgers or the Milwaukee Braves. But with Mays achieving perhaps the best season of
his storied career (.345, 41 home runs, 110 RBIs) and the team's pitchers giving up barely
more than three earned runs a game, the Giants won 97 games and the pennant.*

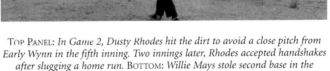

TOP PANEL: *In Game 2, Dusty Rhodes hit the dirt to avoid a close pitch from
Early Wynn in the fifth inning. Two innings later, Rhodes accepted handshakes
after slugging a home run.* BOTTOM: *Willie Mays stole second base in the
10th inning of Game 1. Sam Dente waited for the throw.*

Across town, the Yankees were even better, winning 103 times, a total that would stand up as their best ever in Casey Stengel's 12 years as manager. Yet long before September had run its course, the Yankees' quest for a sixth consecutive world championship was over. They would finish in second place, eight games behind the Cleveland Indians, whose 111 victories were an American League record. That total has since been surpassed twice, but Cleveland's .721 winning percentage remains a league record.

The last team to be as heavily favored in the World Series as the Indians was the 1906 Chicago Cubs, who had won 116 games, but were shockingly dispatched in six games by the crosstown White Sox. The Indians lineup was built around third baseman Al Rosen (24 homers, 102 RBIs) and outfielder Larry Doby (32 homers, 126 RBIs). Four other regulars each had at least 50 RBIs, an impressive total for the era. The top three pitchers — Bob Lemon, Early Wynn and Mike Garcia — had a combined 65-26 record, and 35-year-old Bob Feller won 13 of his 16 decisions.

The Series opened in the Polo Grounds, and the ancient park probably deserved as much credit as any of the Giants for their feats in Game 1, which stunned and demoralized the Indians. First, there was Willie Mays' fabulous catch in the outer reaches of center field in the eighth inning that saved two runs. Then, there was pinch-hitter Dusty Rhodes' three-run home run into the right-field bleachers in the 10th inning that gave the Giants a 5-2 victory. If not for the odd dimensions of the Polo Grounds, Vic Wertz's drive to Mays likely would have been a three-run home run, and Rhodes' home run probably would have been grabbed by the right fielder. But the center-field fence was 483 feet from home plate, and the right-field fence 258 feet.

Rhodes never got more than 244 at-bats in any of his seven seasons with the Giants. But he batted left-handed, had a slight uppercut in his swing and tended to pull the ball — just what God intended for the Polo Grounds. Rhodes struck again in Game 2, entering as a pinch-hitter in the fifth inning and delivering a run-scoring single that tied the score, then hitting a home run in the seventh as the Giants won 3-1. New York had beaten both Lemon and Wynn, each a 23-game winner during the season.

By the time the Series got to Cleveland, the Indians' confidence was flagging badly. Worse for them, Doby had a painful shoulder, and Rosen's leg was so sore that he wasn't in the lineup for Game 3. Rhodes had another pinch-hit that produced two runs in a 6-2 victory. In Game 4, the Giants built a 7-0 lead and won 7-4 to complete the sweep — without needing to summon Rhodes off the bench. He went 4 for 6 with two home runs and seven RBIs in the Series.

It was an improbable and satisfying finish for the Giants in more ways than one, for they were also the kings of New York, despite the Yankees having one of their best seasons. "We showed up those damn Yankees but good!" somebody roared during the raucous clubhouse celebration after Game 4.

1969

NEW YORK METS
~ DEFEATED ~
BALTIMORE ORIOLES

Jerry Koosman delivered a pitch during his 5-3 victory in the decisive Game 5.

Delirious fans stormed the field at Shea Stadium after the Mets won their first Series.

The Mets were Major League Baseball's olive branch to New York City for allowing the Dodgers and the Giants to bolt for the West Coast. National League baseball returned to the Big Apple in 1962, but the Mets played it in such inept fashion that John McGraw surely turned over in his grave on many occasions. "They lost an awful lot of games by one run, which is the mark of a bad team. They also lost innumerable games by 14 runs," wrote Jimmy Breslin, the legendary New York newspaper columnist. These were not "The Boys of Summer" and they certainly were incapable of another "Miracle at Coogan's Bluff." During the first eight years of their existence, the Mets never lost fewer than 89 games, and they finished a combined 288½ games out of first place.

By 1969, however, they had a respectable lineup in place and some fresh-faced pitchers that looked to have bright futures. The best of these were Tom Seaver and Nolan Ryan, as well as Jerry Koosman, Gary Gentry and Tug McGraw. Ryan was still too wild to be trusted with regular work. Seaver, Koosman and Gentry made 102 of the 162 starts and combined for 55 wins. The manager was Gil Hodges, former star first baseman of the Dodgers. A strong, silent type, Hodges knew when to go to the whip and when to pull back with his team as he guided it over a long course.

In mid August, the Mets trailed the first-place Chicago Cubs by 13 games, but with superb pitching and uncanny hitting, they won 34 of their final 44 games and became the first champions of the National League East. By the time they completed a three-game sweep of the Atlanta Braves in the playoffs, the Mets had captured America's imagination. They now were the "Miracle Mets," headed for the World Series and an encounter with the Baltimore Orioles, whose 109 wins were the most in the major leagues since 1954. "We are here to prove there is no Santa Claus," declared Brooks Robinson, the Orioles' brilliant third baseman, who had

grown weary of all the fawning over the Mets.

Indeed, the Series was over quickly. But it was the Mets who won, and they did it in shocking fashion, needing only five games. Mike Cuellar, Baltimore's 23-game winner, beat Seaver 4-1 in Game 1. But the Orioles would score only five more runs.

Koosman won twice, 2-1 in Game 2 and 5-3 in Game 5. Gentry and Ryan combined on a four-hit shutout in Game 3, and Seaver won a 2-1 decision in 10 innings in Game 4. Center fielder Tommy Agee made two incredible catches in Game 3, and right fielder Ron Swoboda saved Seaver's win with a brilliant catch. Al Weis, a career .219 hitter, went 5 for 11. Donn Clendenon, who had retired in February, changed his mind in April and joined the Mets in a June trade, batted .357 and hit three home runs. Whatever the Mets needed, someone usually stepped up and delivered it.

Was it a miracle? "That's one of the great misnomers," Seaver said years later. "If you saw those pitchers and that team, with that manager, you wouldn't call it a miracle at all." No, it was a darned good baseball team that came of age, and it didn't need Santa Claus to make its dreams come true.

Tom Seaver confounded the Orioles for 10 innings in Game 4 and earned a 2-1 victory.

★ ★ ★ ★ ★ ★ ★ ★ ★ ★ ★ ★ ★ ★ ★ ★ ★

1920
BILL WAMBSGANSS' UNASSISTED TRIPLE PLAY

1993
JOE CARTER'S HOME RUN

1921
JOHNNY RAWLINGS' AND GEORGE KELLY'S TRIPLE PLAY

1991
JACK MORRIS' 10-INNING SHUTOUT

1929
HOWARD EHMKE'S 13 STRIKEOUTS

1988
KIRK GIBSON'S HOME RUN

1932
BABE RUTH'S CALLED SHOT

1977
REGGIE JACKSON'S THREE HOME RUNS

1947
AL GIONFRIDDO'S CATCH

1960
BILL MAZEROSKI'S HOME RUN

1954
WILLIE MAYS' CATCH

1975
CARLTON FISK'S HOME RUN

1956
DON LARSEN'S PERFECT GAME

★ ★ ★ ★ ★ ★ ★ ★ ★ ★ ★ ★ ★ ★ ★ ★ ★

AN AMERICAN CLASSIC

GREAT FEATS

THE WORLD SERIES AT 100

1920

BILL WAMBSGANSS' UNASSISTED TRIPLE PLAY

Growing up in the late 1800s and early 1900s, Bill Wambsganss had a passion and a flair for baseball, but that was just child's play. His life's work was mapped out when he was still in the cradle.

T he son of a Lutheran clergyman, Wambsganss, too, would join the ministry and save souls. The dutiful boy went to college, then continued on to divinity school. But he was shy and reticent, and dreaded every occasion when he had to stand at the front and address the class, often freezing up and unable to coax a word from his reluctant mouth. A preacher who can't preach is a bicycle without wheels, and Wambsganss finally found the nerve to inform his father that his calling was in another field or, more precisely, on another field. The father gratefully acknowledged the son's ministry effort. Later, he was ecstatic to learn that young Bill would be joining the Cleveland Indians, the team of his father's longstanding rooting interest.

Bill Wambsganss tagged out Otto Miller to complete his unassisted triple play. Umpire Hank O'Day made the call. Pete Kilduff was around third base before he realized that Wambsganss had doubled him off second base. The third baseman was Larry Gardner, and the third base umpire was Bill Dinneen.

Wambsganss was a shortstop, but the great Ray Chapman held that position in Cleveland, so Wambsganss moved to second base and settled into the Indians' lineup in 1915. He and Chapman quickly became best friends and the best double-play combination in the American League.

Chapman died in August 1920 after a pitched ball crushed his skull. Wambsganss was inconsolable, yet he soldiered on with the Indians, who won the pennant and advanced to the World Series against the Brooklyn Dodgers. While he should have been having the time of his life, the 26-year-old Wambsganss could think only of his fallen buddy. In a soul-bearing, tearful conversation with F. C. Lane, the editor of *Baseball Magazine*, before Game 5, Wambsganss confided that he could not accept Chapman's death and that he feared he was hurting the team with his 2-for-13 batting performance. "Stay with it," Lane advised. "This could very well be your day."

In the fifth inning that day at Cleveland's League Park, the Dodgers had runners on first and second with no outs. With the Indians holding a 7-0 lead, Wambsganss decided that it would be more prudent of him to drop back a lit-tle at his position and guard against a line drive rather than move in closer in hope of making a double play. So he was playing deeper than normal when Clarence Mitchell smashed a line drive toward center field. Wambsganss snatched the ball on the leap, ran to second and touched the bag for a putout on the runner headed for third, then turned and tagged the runner coming from first. It was an unassisted triple play, the rarest feat in Major League Baseball — to be accomplished only 11 times through the 20th century — and it had come in the World Series. Up in the press box, famed sportswriter Ring Lardner pounded into his typewriter, "It was the first time in World Series history that a man named Wambsganss had ever made a triple play assisted by consonants only."

Time tends to make all things better. As the years passed, Wambsganss would break into a broad grin when asked about his small slice of baseball immortality. If the conversation turned to Chapman, Wambsganss would grow silent for a moment, but then he would talk about his long-gone pal, a sad smile warming the memories.

The Game 5 heroes: Wambsganss excelled in the field, and Elmer Smith hit the first grand slam in Series history.

1993 | JOE CARTER'S HOME RUN

There was a clear purpose in Joe Carter's stride as he left the on-deck circle and walked toward home plate to take his at-bat in the bottom of the ninth inning in Game 6 of the 1993 World Series. Two runners were on base, and Carter's team, the Toronto Blue Jays, trailed 6-5. The Philadelphia Phillies needed two outs to extend the Series to the limit. Nobody had ever called Carter a great hitter — his final career batting average was .259 — and many disputed his reputation as a clutch hitter. But these things were undeniable: He had driven home 121 runs during the 1993 season and had amassed 893 RBIs over an eight-year span. By the time he retired in 1998, Carter was one of only nine players in major league history to have achieved at least 100 RBIs in 10 or more seasons, and the other eight were in the Hall of Fame.

On the mound in the ninth inning of Game 6 was Mitch "Wild Thing" Williams, whose pitching performances ranged from brilliant to harrowing, often in the same outing. Williams had been torched for three runs in two-thirds of an inning three days earlier and was the losing pitcher in a 15-14 debacle that ranked as the highest-scoring game in the 532-game history of the World Series.

The count went to two and two, and Williams tried to sneak his signature pitch, a slider, past Carter. But the ball didn't break sharply, and Carter was quick to recognize the mistake. As his hips uncoiled and his arms extended, he felt the familiar jolt and heard the rewarding *thwack!* as the ball flew into the night toward left field. "Ninety-nine times out of 100, I hook that pitch way foul," he would say later. "I don't know why, but, thank God, this one stayed fair." The ball settled into the delirious crowd, and the Blue Jays were the world champions for the second year in a row.

Carter was like a child skipping and dancing on the playground as he circled the bases. He can be excused if he wasn't quite certain how to act, for there wasn't much precedent. The only other man in history who had ended the World Series with a home run was Bill Mazeroski in 1960. The score was tied when Mazeroski hit his home run in the bottom of the ninth inning of Game 7. Carter was the first to bring his team from behind to a Series-ending victory with a single swing of the bat.

Paul Molitor offered a hand to Joe Carter after Carter hit a two-run home run in Game 2. John Olerud was the next batter.

Carter rounded third base and danced toward home plate on his joyous trip around the bases in Game 6.

1921

JOHNNY RAWLINGS' AND GEORGE KELLY'S ❧ TRIPLE PLAY ❧

Johnny Rawlings was the type of ballplayer who could do a respectable job, but any team that was using him regularly as a shortstop or second baseman was probably looking to upgrade at that position. Rawlings lost four jobs on three teams to better players during the course of his career.

George Kelly was among the best ballplayers of his time, although many consider him to be among the least-deserving players enshrined in the Hall of Fame. Kelly, a lean, graceful man who stood six-foot-four and answered to "Highpockets" and "Long George," was a career .297 hitter and a superb fielding first baseman with an exceptionally strong and accurate throwing arm. These two men played side by side in the New York Giants infield for the final three months of the 1921 season — Rawlings had been obtained from the Phillies in a July trade — and did their part to help John McGraw's team win the National League pennant. Kelly's 23 home runs led the NL — one less than the

league record at the time — but it was an embarrassing total, considering that across town a bawdy, rotund slugger named Babe Ruth was mashing 59 for the New York Yankees, almost single-handedly killing baseball's dead ball era.

Those Yankees were in the World Series that year for the first time, the dawn of an American institution. There were a lot of firsts that October. It was the first time the Series matched two New York teams, and it was the first Series to be broadcast on radio. The Polo Grounds was the home for both sides — Yankee Stadium wasn't yet a blueprint — so it was also the first Series to be played in one park. One tradition was on the way out: It was the last Series with a best-of-nine format.

Johnny Rawlings

George Kelly

Rawlings, Bill Cunningham, Irish Meusel and Kelly posed at the Giants' spring training camp in San Antonio, Texas, in 1922.

Ruth got hurt in the Series and was out of the Yankees' lineup for the sixth, seventh and eighth games. Game 8 was a pitchers' duel between Art Nehf of the Giants and Waite Hoyt, the Yankees trailing 1-0 going into the bottom of the ninth. Ruth pinch-hit and grounded out to Kelly. Then Aaron Ward drew a walk. Home Run Baker — what a nickname to have on a team that included Ruth — smashed a hard grounder that appeared certain to reach right field, but Rawlings made a lunging stop and flipped the ball to Kelly at first base for the second out. Ward, meanwhile, had made a left turn at second base and not stopped. Kelly didn't

panic, and his strong, true peg was on the mark to third baseman Frankie Frisch, who slapped a tag on Ward to complete the sterling double play and bring both the game and the Series to a stunning close. (At least Ward didn't have to answer to George Steinbrenner for his gaffe.)

A year later, the Giants had upgraded at second base. Rawlings was on the bench and later off to his sixth professional team. Kelly remained, and along with Frisch at second, Dave Bancroft at shortstop and Heinie Grohl at third, formed what came to be regarded as the best infield in Giants history.

1991

JACK MORRIS' 10-INNING SHUTOUT

When he joined his hometown Minnesota Twins in 1991, Jack Morris was almost 36. His best days as a major league pitcher appeared to be behind him. He had won more games in the 1980s than any other pitcher, but in his final two seasons with the Detroit Tigers, his employer for the first 14 years of his career, he had lost 32 games and won only 21. Morris, though, still had the fierce competitive streak that had long marked him as a number one starter, the kind of pitcher who causes his team's confidence to soar when he is on the mound.

The Twins in 1991 would become the first American League team to go from last place to first place in successive seasons, and Morris was right in the thick of the dramatic turnaround, winning 18 of his 30 decisions and posting a 3.43 ERA. It can be argued that both Scott Erickson (20-9, 3.18 ERA) and Kevin Tapani (16-9, 2.99 ERA) were better pitchers for the Twins than Morris. But when manager Tom Kelly set up his three-man pitching rotation for postseason play, Morris was first on the list, because that's who Kelly most wanted on the mound should the Twins play a Game 7. They did, facing the Atlanta Braves in the World Series.

Morris, who had won two games in the League Championship Series and pitched brilliantly in his first two starts in the World Series, climbed the Metrodome mound to decide one of the most hotly contested Series in history. Morris and his counterpart on the Braves, 24-year-old John Smoltz, a Michigan native who had idolized Morris during Morris' days with the Tigers, took turns retiring the side without giving up a run. The Braves loaded the bases in the eighth inning and would have scored but for a base-running gaffe by Lonnie Smith. The Twins loaded the bases in their half of the eighth. Smoltz deferred to the bullpen, which blunted the rally.

Morris retired the Braves without incident in the ninth to keep the game scoreless. He returned to the dugout, where Kelly was waiting to tell the pitcher that he was taking him out of the game. The defiant Morris would have none of it. Kelly finally relented, saying, "Okay, what the hell — it's just a game." Yeah, right. Again in the 10th, the Braves couldn't crack Morris. The Twins finally scored in the bottom of the 10th and won the Series for the second time in five years.

Morris had the signature game of his illustrious career, a seven-hitter over 10 innings in which he bent several times, but never broke. Three other pitchers had achieved shutouts in Game 7 — Johnny Podres in 1955, Ralph Terry in 1962 and Sandy Koufax in 1965 — but none had done it over 10 innings. (Christy Mathewson in 1912 was the only other pitcher to work more than nine innings in the deciding game of a Series, but he had lost.) Given the circumstances and the stakes, Morris had fashioned one of the most impressive pitching performances in history.

1929 | HOWARD EHMKE'S 13 STRIKEOUTS

Howard Ehmke had accounted well for himself in the major leagues. He once had been a 20-game winner for a last-place team, twice had exceeded 300 innings in a season. He pitched a no-hitter in 1923 and would have had another in his next start except for an official scorer's decision that went against him. Ehmke stood six-foot-three and whipped the ball toward home plate with a sidearm motion, his long right arm coming right out of the white, short-sleeved shirts in the center-field bleachers on those days when the park was full, and vexing many a right-handed hitter.

By 1929, Ehmke was 35, just a bit player on the Philadelphia Athletics, relying on off-speed offerings and guile. He went 7-2 that year, but pitched in only 11 games. Connie Mack, the A's longtime owner and manager, summoned Ehmke one day late in the season, intending to release the pitcher. The A's had a powerful grip on first place in the American League, cruising toward a 104-win season and their first pennant in 15 years. The distraught Ehmke begged Mack not to quash what surely would be the pitcher's final chance to make the World Series, and the thoughtful old gentleman relented.

It struck Mack that just maybe Ehmke could be useful. Over in the National League, the Chicago Cubs were certain pennant winners, too. Mack, aware that everyone in the Chicago lineup except Charlie Grimm batted right-handed, sent Ehmke out to scout the Cubs on the sly. Mack told Ehmke he was considering using him in Game 1 of the Series, then warned the pitcher, "Don't even tell your wife about this."

So when the Series began at Wrigley Field, it wasn't 24-game-winner George Earnshaw, 20-game-winner Lefty Grove or even 18-game-winner Rube Walberg on the mound for the A's. Ehmke went out there with the pride and resolve of an old warrior who knew he was on his final battlefield. Given the stage he was on, he pitched the game of his life, confounding the Cubs inning after inning with slow stuff and breaking stuff, dotting the corners, tying the hitters in knots. The National League champions, a .303-hitting team that year, managed eight hits. The Cubs scored an unearned run in the ninth to cut the A's lead to 3-1 and had two men on base with two outs. But the amazing Ehmke, still something left in his old hose, ended the game by striking out Chick Tolson. It was Ehmke's 13th K, breaking a 23-year-old Series record. Of all those there that day, the great sportswriter Grantland Rice best put in words what they witnessed. "The long, lazy right arm of Howard Ehmke," Rice wrote, "fell across the back of the Cubs like a whip."

The A's won the Series in five games. Ehmke pitched once more, but was not effective. He would never win again in the major leagues, making just three appearances in 1930 before being released and slipping into retirement, content in knowing that he had made the most of a chance he almost didn't get.

1988 | KIRK GIBSON'S ~HOME RUN~

WORLD SERIES PINCH-HIT HOME RUNS

	YEAR	G	I		YEAR	G	
Jim Leyritz, New York Yankees	1999	4	8	**Elston Howard,** New York Yankees	1960	1	9
Ed Sprague, Toronto Blue Jays	1992	2	9	**Chuck Essegian,** Los Angeles Dodgers	1959	6	9
Chili Davis, Minnesota Twins	1991	3	8	**Chuck Essegian,** Los Angeles Dodgers	1959	2	7
Bill Bathe, San Francisco Giants	1989	3	9	**Bob Cerv,** New York Yankees	1955	5	7
Kirk Gibson, Los Angeles Dodgers	1988	1	9	**Hank Majeski,** Cleveland Indians	1954	4	5
Jay Johnstone, Los Angeles Dodgers	1981	4	6	**Dusty Rhodes,** New York Giants	1954	1	10
Bernie Carbo, Boston Red Sox	1975	6	8	**George Shuba,** Brooklyn Dodgers	1953	1	6
Bernie Carbo, Boston Red Sox	1975	3	7	**Johnny Mize,** New York Yankees	1952	3	
Johnny Blanchard, New York Yankees	1961	3	8	**Yogi Berra,** New York Yankees	1947	3	7

Kirk Gibson never led his league in anything. He never hit as many as 30 home runs in a season, never had as many as 100 RBIs, never was a .300 hitter. He never played in an All-Star Game. Yet Gibson was as respected as any ballplayer of his era, if not always by fans and media, then certainly by those he played with and against. "He's a ballplayer's ballplayer," Sparky Anderson, Gibson's manager with the Detroit Tigers, once said. "When he walks through that clubhouse door, everyone knows he's there. He comes to play and is ready to fight, down and dirty, day after day."

G ibson was an all-American wide receiver at Michigan State University and had the talent to play in the National Football League. Instead, he chose baseball, but it wouldn't do him justice to merely say that he played the game. Rather, he attacked the game, calling upon the same fierce intensity and raw emotion that had fueled his fury in football. That reckless abandon often caused Gibson physical damage, but his general rule was that if he could make it onto the field on his own power, he could play.

That resolve resulted in one of the most dramatic home runs in World Series history. Gibson had joined the Los Angeles Dodgers in January 1988, and nine months later the team was in the World Series for the first time in 10 years. Gibson, who would be the National League's Most Valuable Player that season, had only four hits in the League Championship Series against the New York Mets, but one was a 12th-inning home run that won Game 4 and another a three-run homer that helped win Game 5. But he was a physical wreck by this time, his hamstrings and knees so sore that he wasn't expected to be able to play in the Series against the heavily favored Oakland Athletics, who had won 104 games during the season.

Game 1 was at Dodger Stadium, and Gibson watched most of it on a television set in the clubhouse trainer's room, his legs packed in ice. The A's took a 4-3 lead into the ninth inning. "I'm sitting there in my shorts, and something in my head says, 'It's time to get dressed,'" Gibson said. No sooner had he put on his uniform and hobbled out to the dugout than manager Tommy Lasorda told him to grab his bat. Dennis Eckersley, the game's best relief pitcher, had gotten two outs, but then he had walked a Dodger.

A day earlier, Gibson had tried to swing a bat, but the pain was too much to bear. He felt a little better now, and after fouling off the first two pitches, he worked the count to three and two. Eckersley then delivered a slider that didn't break properly. Gibson connected solidly and drove the ball over the right-field fence — a home run from a virtual cripple that came like a bolt of lightning and brought the game to a stunning and unexpected end.

Gibson limped around the bases, pumping his right arm in exultation, and then went back to the training room for the rest of the Series. The Dodgers beat the demoralized A's in five games for the world championship. At the end of the century, Gibson's homer was voted the greatest moment in Los Angeles sports history.

By the end of the 1932 season, Babe Ruth was running on fumes. Years of overindulging on hot dogs, hooch, Havanas and hotties had taken a toll on the famed Bambino. He was 37 years old and carried an ever-expanding spare tire around his midsection. Not to say that he was no longer a productive player; a .341 average, 41 homers and 137 RBIs for 1932 tell otherwise. But those were hardly Ruthian numbers. The end was approaching — Ruth had only three seasons and 62 home runs (of his career 714) left in him — yet the Babe was still capable of performance that spit in the face of mortality. What he did — or didn't do — in Game 3 of the 1932 World Series further embellished his personal mythology.

The Yankees won 107 games in 1932 and were heavy favorites to defeat the Chicago Cubs in the World Series. The Cubs had lost their shortstop, Billy Jurges, to injury in August, yet they had found an able replacement in their farm system. He was Mark Koenig,

1932 | BABE RUTH'S ⊰CALLED SHOT⊱

who batted .353 and played superbly in the stretch run — the same Mark Koenig who had been the Yankees' regular shortstop from 1926 through 1929 and a popular teammate. Cubs players, for their own reasons, voted to give Koenig only a half share of their Series money.

That didn't sit well with the Yankees, who rallied in support of their old teammate. Ruth led the verbal charge. "Hey, you lousy bunch of cheapskates," boomed the Babe as the Cubs filed onto the field at Yankee Stadium prior to Game 1. And after pumping a dozen batting-practice pitches into the Wrigley Field bleachers prior to Game 3, Ruth cracked, "I'd play for half my salary if I could hit in this dump all my life." Cubs players, in turn, taunted Ruth throughout the Series ("I'd never known there were so many cuss words or so many ways of stringing them together," said Yankees third baseman Joe Sewell) and their fans allegedly spat on Ruth's wife. A Chicago newspaper, hitting below the belt, wrote of the Yankees: "One of their outfielders is a fat, elderly party who must wear corsets to avoid immodest jiggling, and cannot waddle for fly balls, nor stoop for grounders."

Lou Gehrig had a hand for Babe Ruth after Ruth hit his "called shot" and rounded the bases in Game 3. The catcher was Gabby Hartnett, and the umpire was Roy Van Graflan.

By Game 3, the Babe had pretty much had it with the Cubs. He popped a three-run homer in the first inning, and the score was tied 4-4 when he stepped into the batter's box in the fifth. After the first pitch from Charlie Root, a called strike, Ruth lifted his right forefinger and pointed. After another called strike, the Babe lifted two fingers and pointed. On Root's next offering, Ruth connected and sent a majestic drive that soared well over the center-field fence and was regarded as the longest home run ever struck at Wrigley. The Yankees won that game, and a day later they completed a four-game sweep of the Cubs.

Did Ruth actually point twice to the center-field bleachers to indicate that was where he intended to hit the ball? Did he call his shot? There is no definitive answer, and the legend made this home run one of the most memorable in history. Some historians claim that Ruth was motioning toward his hecklers in the Cubs' dugout or toward Root on the mound. The "called shot" took on a life of its own in the newspapers, and the cagey Ruth knew he couldn't make the story any better if he talked about it, so he kept his trap shut. When asked about it over the years, the Babe usually shrugged and said, "Why don't you read the papers? It's all right there."

Reggie Jackson admired the flight of his third home run in Game 6.
OPPOSITE PAGE: *Jackson connected against Elias Sosa for his second home run.*

ONE SERIES
HOME RUNS

	YEAR	NO.	G		YEAR	NO.	G		YEAR	NO.	G
REGGIE JACKSON	1977	5	6	LENNY DYKSTRA	1993	4	6	DUKE SNIDER	1955	4	7
LOU GEHRIG	1928	4	6	HANK BAUER	1958	4	7	DUKE SNIDER	1952	4	7
WILLIE AIKENS	1980	4	6	BABE RUTH	1926	4	7	GENE TENACE	1972	4	7

1977 | REGGIE JACKSON'S THREE HOME RUNS

The first chance Reggie Jackson got to choose which baseball team he would play for, he headed for New York City to wear the pinstripes of the Yankees.

It was the biggest city and the most famous team, and the egomaniacal Jackson would not settle for anything less. He bragged that once he got to New York, they'd name a candy bar after him — and they did. He took a place in Manhattan rather than going to the suburbs, where the rest of the Yankees lived, and relished the chance to ride in elevators with moguls, captains of industry, and others in three-piece suits. "In the building I live in on Park Avenue, there are 10 people who could buy the Yankees — but none of them could hit the ball out of Yankee Stadium," Reggie would say smugly.

That first season in New York, 1977, proved to be considerably more difficult than Reggie might ever have imagined. He alienated teammates early by declaring that he was "the straw that stirred the drink," which was taken as an insult to the team's highly respected captain, Thurman Munson. He clashed often with the Yankees' volatile and intemperate manager, Billy Martin. Jackson craved adulation, lived for it, but, much to his chagrin, he found that it didn't come easily in New York. He was often miserable, yet he set his jaw and stubbornly persevered. At season's end, he had 32 home runs, 110 RBIs, and 20 game-winning hits — one of his finest years.

The Yankees had hired Jackson because the previous year they had gone to the World Series and lost, and team owner George Steinbrenner was not going to allow that to happen again. This time, the Yankees took a 3-2 Series lead over the Los Angeles Dodgers. Game 6 was in Yankee Stadium, and baseball fans around the world were about to witness the greatest performance ever by a batter in a Series game, presented by a proud man who came to New York to prove that he was indeed as big as any Mr. Big.

After walking in his first at-bat, Jackson launched home runs on the first pitch in each of his next three trips to the plate. The third home run was a soaring shot that landed beyond the center-field fence, some 450 feet from home plate. Jackson swaggered around the bases, and at last he had an adoring audience. The huge crowd chanted "Reggie! Reggie! Reggie!" and was deafening in its roar. Soon thereafter, the Yankees won the World Series for the first time since 1962.

Jackson hit five home runs in the Series, a record. The last four came in four official at-bats, going back to the eighth inning of Game 5. The big man lived for the biggest stage, and his performance usually merited the loudest cheers. His batting average during his six World Series is 95 points better than his season average (.357 to .262) and his slugging percentage of .755 is a Series record.

1947 | AL GIONFRIDDO'S CATCH

Al Gionfriddo probably would not have played in the major leagues had it not been for World War II. As more and more players marched off to war, teams had to dip deeper into the talent pool for replacements, and that's why Gionfriddo was able to find work with the Pittsburgh Pirates late in the 1944 season. Compactly built at five-foot-six and 165 pounds, Gionfriddo was both fast and quick, traits that served him well when he was on base and in the outfield. But he offered little with his bat, showing only a .266 average and two home runs in his 580 at-bats in the major leagues.

As players returned from the war, Gionfriddo played less and less frequently. During the 1947 season, he was so firmly stuck to the Brooklyn Dodgers' bench that team president Branch Rickey decided to release him. Some claimed that Burt Shotton, the Dodgers manager, didn't even know Gionfriddo's name, noting that he always referred to him as "the little Italian fella." But Shotton had a soft spot for Gionfriddo, and he persuaded Rickey that the player was worth keeping as a pinch-hitter, pinch-runner and late-inning defensive replacement. Still, Gionfriddo did little but sit that summer, appearing in only 37 games and hitting but .177 in 62 at-bats.

The Dodgers made it to the World Series for the first time in six years, and the Yankees for the first time in four years. Gionfriddo played a bit role in Game 4, entering as a pinch-runner in the bottom of the ninth inning, stealing a base and scoring on Cookie Lavagetto's famous two-run double that gave Brooklyn a 3-2 victory.

Two days later, Gionfriddo arrived at Yankee Stadium still an obscure ballplayer. By the time he left late that afternoon, he had done something that baseball fans would be asking him about

until the day he died 56 years later at age 81. The Dodgers had an 8-5 lead and were about to take the field for the bottom of the sixth inning when Shotton told Gionfriddo to go to left field as a replacement for Eddie Miksis. Soon, the Yankees had two runners on base and the great Joe DiMaggio at the plate.

If you had been listening to the game on the Dodgers' radio station, here's what you would have heard from Red Barber, the team's legendary broadcaster: "Here's the pitch. Swung on, belted! It's a long one, deep to left center! Back goes Gionfriddo! Back, back, back, back, back, back! He makes a one-handed catch against the bullpen! Oh, doctor!"

Gionfriddo had lost his cap while racing for the ball; he leaped and made the catch near the 415-foot marker — the ball would not have cleared the fence, but Gionfriddo saved two runs. DiMaggio, gliding into second base, kicked at the dirt in frustration, a public display of emotion so rare for him that it has become almost as memorable as Gionfriddo's catch.

The Dodgers won 8-6 to live another day, but the Yankees won Game 7. Gionfriddo, who went 0 for 3 in the Series, watched that one from the bench, and never played in the major leagues again. He is the most famous position player in Series history who never got a hit.

Joe DiMaggio (left) and other somber Yankees headed for the clubhouse after they lost Game 6.

Pee Wee Reese planted a kiss on the cheek of Al Gionfriddo in the Dodgers clubhouse.

GAME-ENDING
HOME RUNS

	YEAR	G	I		YEAR	G	I
*BILL MAZEROSKI	1960	7	9	CHAD CURTIS	1999	3	10
*JOE CARTER	1993	6	9	MICKEY MANTLE	1964	3	9
KIRBY PUCKETT	1991	6	11	DUSTY RHODES	1954	1	10
CARLTON FISK	1975	6	12	TOMMY HENRICH	1949	1	9
EDDIE MATHEWS	1957	4	10	KIRK GIBSON	1988	1	9
MARK McGWIRE	1988	3	9	*ENDED WORLD SERIES			

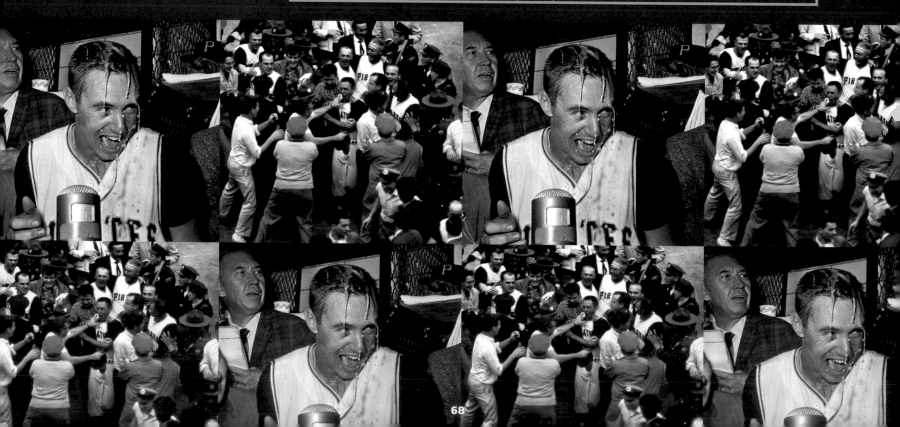

1960 | BILL MAZEROSKI'S HOME RUN

Bill Mazeroski packed 185 pounds on his sturdy five-foot-eleven frame. Strong through the wrists and arms, he could put a jolt into a baseball when he connected with a bat. He hoped to be a great hitter, but his legacy would be his defense. Many regard him as the best fielding second baseman in Major League Baseball history.

Much of Pittsburgh seemed to be waiting for Bill Mazeroski by the time he rounded the bases and approached home plate.

As a hitter, Mazeroski probably was a little too strong for his own good. The outfield fences tantalized him, but he didn't really have enough power to reach them consistently. In his third season, Maz slugged 19 home runs, a considerable number for a second baseman in the late 1950s. Flush with long-ball fever, he swung harder the next season, but managed only seven home runs, and his batting averaged dropped 34 points. It was still plummeting in the summer of 1960 when George Sisler, the Pittsburgh Pirates batting coach, took Maz aside and recommended that he make some adjustments.

Mazeroski's batting strategy had been to pull pitches and aim for the left-field fence. Sisler, who had been a .340 hitter in his day, persuaded Mazeroski to stand deeper in the batter's box, wait longer on the pitch, and swing just to make contact. It worked. Mazeroski was batting .237 in early August, but he was up to .273 by the end of the season and had 11 home runs and 64 RBIs — easily the best production among National League second basemen.

The Pirates made the World Series in 1960 for the first time in 33 years, but they weren't given much chance against the New York Yankees, a team that had won seven of the previous 11 Series. The Pirates, however, persisted. The Series was tied after six games, and Game 7 was tied 9-9 going into the bottom of the ninth inning at Forbes Field.

The first batter for the Pirates was Mazeroski, who had hit a two-run homer in Game 1 and had driven in two runs in Game 5, both Pirates victories. Ralph Terry's first pitch was called a ball. He delivered again, and this one came in belt-high. Mazeroski breathed deeply, kept his weight back and then swung free and easy, just as Sisler had taught him. The ball shot off Mazeroski's bat into the late afternoon shadows on an arc for left field, and disappeared over the ivy-covered wall. Of all the home runs in history, it was the first one that had ended Game 7 of a World Series.

125PX

49

125PX

1954 | WILLIE MAYS' ❦ CATCH ❧

Willie Mays would play Major League Baseball for 22 years and hit more home runs than anyone else in history except Babe Ruth and Hank Aaron. But in Mays' case, statistics are a hollow measurement of the total ballplayer. Listen to Leo Durocher, Mays' manager and protector for the first five years of his career: "If somebody came up and hit .450, stole 100 bases and performed a miracle in the field every day, I'd still look you in the eye and say Willie was better. He could do the five things you have to do to be a superstar: hit, hit with power, run, throw and field. And he had that other magic ingredient that turns a superstar into a super superstar: He lit up the room when he came in."

As the 1954 season ran its course, evidence mounted daily that the 23-year-old Mays was to be a ballplayer for the ages. His capacity, energy and enthusiasm for the game seemed to have no bounds, and all of it was reaching full bloom that summer as Mays led the New York Giants to an unexpected National League pennant. By the end of July, he had hit 36 home runs and was on pace to break Babe Ruth's record. But Durocher told Mays that the team would be better off if he hit for a higher average, so Mays adjusted his batting style and hit .345, good for his only batting title. He also had 41 home runs and 110 RBIs, ran the bases flawlessly and made spectacular plays seem routine in his position in center field at the horseshoe-shaped Polo Grounds, which had the largest outfield expanse in the major leagues.

Mays was such a complete player that he could go hitless and still alter the course of a game. That is precisely what he did in Game 1 of the 1954 World Series against the Cleveland Indians, who had set an American League record by winning 111 games. In the eighth inning, with runners on first and second, no outs and the score tied 2-2, Vic Wertz of the Indians crushed a drive toward the outer reaches of center field at the Polo Grounds. At the crack of the bat, Mays spun 90 degrees and was on a dead sprint, racing perhaps 75 yards to the warning track in right center and catching the ball over his left shoulder.

"I knew I'd catch this ball — that wasn't the problem," Mays said later. "The problem was Larry Doby on second base. On a deep fly to center field at the Polo Grounds, a runner could score all the way from second. I've done that myself, and more than once. So if I make the catch, which I will, and Larry scores from second, they still get the run that puts them ahead." Mays stopped dead in his tracks after catching the ball, twirled around, planted on his left leg for momentum and fired a laser beam–like strike to the cutoff man. The runner on second managed to get to third, but the runner on first stayed put.

The Giants won 5-2 and went on to sweep the stunned Indians in four games, but the legend of the Series forever remains a catch and throw that is, if not the best defensive play in history, certainly the most famous. Today, it might just be another "web gem" on *Baseball Tonight*. But in 1954, America was entering the television age, and Mays' incredible feat played out on grainy black-and-white screens all over the country, astounding fans far beyond the ballpark.

1975 | CARLTON FISK'S HOME RUN

I t was only right that Carlton Fisk should hit one of the most memorable home runs in history, a shot into the midnight sky at Boston's Fenway Park during the 1975 World Series. He deserved a niche in the game's lore for his long and distinguished service to Major League Baseball in a playing career that spanned four decades. It began when the Vietnam War was raging and was still going strong when the Gulf War broke out. His 20-year run as a regular catcher, first for the Boston Red Sox and then the Chicago White Sox, is the longest in history. Most catchers are worn out by the time they reach 33, but Fisk was just getting his second wind at that age. When he was finally shown the door at age 45, he had caught more games than anyone else in history, hit more home runs than

any other catcher and hit more home runs after turning 40 than anyone else.

Tall and handsome, Fisk had a patrician look about him, but in reality he was from hard-working New England stock. Fiercely dedicated, Fisk trained fanatically, often spending an hour and a half lifting weights after he had caught a nine-inning game. He considered baseball to be a calling rather than a job and believed that the chosen ones were duty-bound to play the game with honor and respect. When he encountered anything less, Fisk became baseball's sternest sergeant at arms.

One day in New York, 22-year-old "Neon" Deion Sanders of the Yankees, a two-sport player earning millions, hit a pop-up and walked toward first base.

The 42-year-old Fisk, who was behind the plate, stalked angrily toward Sanders, and shouted, "Run it out, you piece of shit!" Approaching the plate for his next at-bat, Sanders felt the piercing glare of Fisk and muttered something about slavery having been abolished. The boiling Fisk retorted that Hank Aaron and Willie Mays ran out their pop-ups when they played, and that Sanders, less than a month in the big leagues, damn well would do it, too. Fisk got into Sanders' face and shouted, "Let me tell you something, you little cocksucker. There's a right way and a wrong way to play this game. You're playing it the wrong way — and the rest of us don't like it!"

Some consider that encounter to be Fisk's greatest legacy, a lesson for all in doing the right thing. Others opt for Fisk's 1975 home run off Pat Darcy of the Cincinnati Reds that brought Game 6 to a stunning end in the bottom of the 12th inning. Fisk dropped his bat, hopped sideways a few steps toward first base and frantically waved his extended arms from left to right as to direct the long fly ball that he had just hit to land in fair territory. The ball struck the mesh attached to the right side of the left-field foul pole — a home run for Fisk and a 7-6 victory for the Red Sox. *TV Guide* selected the television footage of Fisk's dramatics as the number one video sports moment of the 20th century. The best part for Fisk was that he was just 27; there was still much baseball to be played.

27 UP; 27 DOWN | *Here is the Brooklyn Dodgers lineup that Don Larsen faced on October 8, 1956, and their statistics for the season. Reese, Snider, Robinson and Campanella are in the Hall of Fame.*

Don Larsen was never more valuable to the New York Yankees than on a December day in 1959 when he and three others were traded to the Kansas City Athletics for Roger Maris and two others. Maris was the American League's Most Valuable Player the following season, and a year later he broke Babe Ruth's record for most home runs in a season. However, for one day in his five seasons with the Yankees, Larsen was the greatest pitcher on earth, the equal of any of the legendary hurlers in Major League Baseball history. On October 8, 1956, he pitched the only perfect game in World Series history.

Some things simply cannot be explained, and this was one of them. Larsen had talent, but he was never particularly dedicated to his craft. He loved the nightlife and, much to his delight, found that "last call" in New York City never came. Jimmy Dykes, his manager in Baltimore before he joined the Yankees, once said, "The only thing Larsen fears is sleep." Larsen's nickname among teammates was "Gooneybird," for his happy-go-lucky approach to life. Besides carousing, his great passion was reading comic books. Larsen so loved one pulp fiction character, "The Nightrider," that he took to calling himself the same.

Larsen was a 21-game loser for Baltimore in

Don Larsen threw 97 pitches in Game 5, and none of them were hit safely. Afterward, Yogi Berra leaped into the perfect pitcher's arms.

	HR	RBI	BA		HR	RBI	BA
JUNIOR GILLIAM 2B	6	43	.300	SANDY AMOROS LF	16	58	.260
PEE WEE REESE SS	9	46	.257	CARL FURILLO RF	21	83	.289
DUKE SNIDER CF	43	101	.292	ROY CAMPANELLA C	20	73	.219
JACKIE ROBINSON 3B	10	43	.275	SAL MAGLIE P	0	2	.129
GIL HODGES 1B	32	87	.265	DALE MITCHELL PH	0	7	.204

1954, but he found some success in New York, going 30-11 in his first three seasons with the Yankees. Those were great teams, all pennant winners, and Larsen was never higher than fourth in the pitching rotation. His 11 victories in 1956 (against five losses) was the high mark of his 14-year career which ended with an 81-91 record. Larsen started Game 2 of the 1956 Series against the Brooklyn Dodgers, but he failed to hold a 6-0 lead and was out of the game in the second inning.

Three days later, Yankees manager Casey Stengel sent Larsen to the mound again, and this time the 27-year-old righthander stepped out of his mortality. Inning by inning, he retired the Dodgers in order, vexing a lineup that included four players who would make it to the Hall of Fame — Jackie Robinson, Pee Wee Reese, Duke Snider and Roy Campanella. Larsen's teammates gave him a 2-0 lead, then watched in bewilderment and awe, waiting for him to crash.

Instead, the ninth inning arrived, and Larsen dispatched Brooklyn's 25th and 26th batters of the day. Up next came pinch-hitter Dale Mitchell. Ball one. Strike one. Strike two. On the next pitch, Mitchell started to swing, but pulled back. Umpire Babe Pinelli, however, shot the index finger of his right hand into the air, signaling strike three and the completion of what would be one of only 14 perfect games in the 20th century.

★ ★ ★ ★ ★ ★ ★ ★ ★ ★ ★ ★ ★ ★ ★

1909
BABE ADAMS, PITTSBURGH PIRATES

1990
BILLY HATCHER, CINCINNATI REDS

1914
HANK GOWDY, BOSTON BRAVES

1983
RICK DEMPSEY, BALTIMORE ORIOLES

1931
PEPPER MARTIN, ST. LOUIS CARDINALS

1978
BRIAN DOYLE AND BUCKY DENT, NEW YORK YANKEES

1953
BILLY MARTIN, NEW YORK YANKEES

1972
GENE TENACE, OAKLAND ATHLETICS

1960
BOBBY RICHARDSON, NEW YORK YANKEES

1969
AL WEIS, NEW YORK METS

★ ★ ★ ★ ★ ★ ★ ★ ★ ★ ★ ★ ★ ★ ★

AN AMERICAN CLASSIC

UNLIKELY HEROES

THE WORLD SERIES AT 100

BABE Adams

1909 | PITTSBURGH PIRATES

O n the eve of the 1909 World Series, Fred Clarke, manager of the National League champion Pittsburgh Pirates, received distressing news. The Pirates' best pitcher, 25-game winner Howie Camnitz, had been diagnosed with a severe case of tonsillitis and likely would be unavailable. This was a harsh blow for the Pirates, who had won 110 games — second-best NL total of the 20th century — but were up against the Detroit Tigers, the American League champion three times running, and Detroit's player for the ages, Ty Cobb, a .377 hitter with 76 stolen bases that season.

Clarke could have opened the Series with 22-game-winner Vic Willis, 19-game-winner Lefty Leifield, or even 13-game-winner Nick Maddox. Instead, heeding the suggestion of NL president John Heydler, Clarke sent 12-game winner Charles "Babe" Adams, a 27-year-old rookie, to the mound for Game 1. Heydler had observed that Adams and Washington Senators pitcher Dolly Gray had strikingly similar pitching styles, and Gray had been successful against the Tigers that season.

The six-foot, 185-pound Adams, an Indiana farm boy, hardly cut an imposing figure on the pitcher's mound. He didn't throw particularly hard and gave up more hits than the norm for starting pitchers of that era. But even as a rookie, Adams had uncanny control of his pitches. If Greg Maddux were a clone, he surely would be from Adams' DNA. Adams was the second-best control artist of the 20th century, walking 1.29 batters on average per nine innings. Incredibly, the number one man on that list, Deacon Phillippe (1.18 walks per nine innings) was also on the 1909 Pirates team, but at 37 he was on the downslope of his career.

Given Adams' penchant for throwing strikes, it didn't bode well for the Pirates when he walked two of the first three Tigers in Game 1. But Adams stepped off the mound, drew a long breath and collected himself, and stopped the Tigers in their tracks the rest of the game, winning 4-1. He won Game 5 by an 8-4 score, walking one and striking out eight. On two days' rest, Adams took the mound for Game 7 and pitched a six-hitter. The Pirates had an 8-0 victory and their first world championship, and Adams was the first pitcher to win three games in a seven-game Series. More than 90 years later, no other rookie had replicated the feat. For the Series, Adams had a 1.33 ERA, and six walks and 11 strikeouts in 27 innings. The immortal Cobb solved him for only 1 hit in 11 at-bats.

Adams was the Pirates' top pitcher for the next six seasons. He continued to pitch until 1926, finishing with a 194-140 record. After baseball, he took up farming in northeast Missouri. A nearby portion of U.S. Highway 136 is named "Babe Adams Highway" in his honor. It is presumed that the stretch of asphalt, like Adams' pitches, runs true.

BILLY Hatcher

1990 | CINCINNATI REDS ❖

Billy Hatcher took a robust swing one day in 1987 and smashed his bat squarely into the baseball. Unfortunately for Hatcher, the barrel of the bat split open upon contact and umpires found that the bat had been hollowed out and stuffed with cork, a violation of Major League Baseball rules. Hatcher did what any self-respecting hitter would have done: He laid the blame on a pitcher.

Hatcher claimed that he had borrowed the bat from Dave Smith, unaware that Smith had added cork so that he might hit batting-practice pitches over the wall and impress onlookers. Nevertheless, Major League Baseball still held Hatcher responsible for the violation and suspended the Houston Astros outfielder for 10 days.

Except for the bat-corking incident and a 14th-inning home run in Game 6 of the 1986 National League Championship Series, Hatcher did little to distinguish himself during his first six seasons in the major leagues. In 1990, he joined the Cincinnati Reds — his fourth team — and helped them win the National League pennant with his steady play in center field and .276 average and 30 stolen bases from the number two position in the batting order. In August, he tied a major league record by hitting four doubles in a game.

The Reds weren't given much of a chance in the World Series against the mighty Oakland Athletics, who were there for the third consecutive year and had won 103 games in 1990. (The Reds won 91.) But no one expected the Series to be four days old before Oakland's vaunted pitching staff managed to get an out against Hatcher.

Great hitters talk about getting locked into a zone in which every pitch that comes their way looks as big and tantalizing as a grapefruit. Hatcher must have been seeing watermelons. He went 3 for 3 and drew a walk in Game 1, and then went 4 for 4 and drew another walk in Game 2. That was seven consecutive hits in one Series, a feat that had never previously been accomplished. (Thurman Munson of the New York Yankees had seven consecutive hits during the 1976 and 1977 Series.)

Hatcher had two more hits in Game 3, and had barely settled into the batter's box for Game 4 when Dave Stewart's fastball caught him flush on the hand. Forced to the bench, Hatcher watched the rest of the Reds' 2-1 victory that completed a stunning four-game sweep of the A's. Hatcher's contribution: 9 hits in 12 at-bats, a .750 average that broke Babe Ruth's 62-year-old Series record. He also scored six of the Reds' 22 runs. Surprisingly, the A's never questioned whether Hatcher might be using one of Dave Smith's bat.

ONE SERIES BATTING AVERAGE

	YEAR	AVG.	H	AB	G		YEAR	AVG.	H	AB	G
BILLY HATCHER	1990	.750	9	12	4	CHRIS SABO	1990	.563	9	16	4
BABE RUTH	1928	.625	10	16	4	HANK GOWDY	1914	.545	6	11	4
RICKY LEDEE	1998	.600	6	10	4	LOU GEHRIG	1928	.545	6	11	4

HANK Gowdy

The kid was a leader, and Stallings knew a thing or two about that quality, having grown up the son of a Confederate Army general. It was 1912, and both men were in the employ of the Buffalo Bisons. Hank Gowdy was the catcher, back in the minors after bit roles in the major leagues for three seasons. Stallings was the manager, cooling his heels and waiting for a chance to manage his fourth major league team.

When the Boston Braves came for Stallings a year later, he made it a point to keep up with Gowdy's progress. Stallings, who had a fine reputation for judging baseball talent, deemed the kid ready for the Braves' lineup in 1914, and the two set off on what was for all the principals involved among the most satisfying seasons in Major League Baseball history.

With Gowdy behind the plate, finessing what essentially was a three-man pitching staff, the once-lowly Braves won the National League pennant and advanced to the World Series against Connie Mack's mighty Philadelphia Athletics. Gowdy was a .243 hitter that season and would be a .270 hitter for his 17 major league seasons. Yet over a five-day span in October 1914, he played far above that level, probably as magnificently as anyone ever has played on baseball's

grand stage. As the Braves fashioned an improbable four-game sweep of the A's, the 25-year-old Gowdy batted .545 and reached base in nine of his 14 at-bats.

Game 3 was a test of the Braves' mettle, and Gowdy made sure they passed. The score was 2-2 after nine innings, and the A's scored twice in the 10th. Gowdy led off the bottom of the 10th with a home run, and the Braves scored again to tie the score. In the 12th, Gowdy doubled to left field and later scored the winning run on a wild throw. A day later, the stunned A's were done for the year.

Gowdy also lived on the other end of success. In 1924, playing for the New York Giants, he caught his foot in his mask and failed to catch a pop-up in the 12th inning of Game 7 of the World Series. "It held me like a bear trap," Gowdy said sadly. Given another chance by the error, Muddy Ruel doubled and later scored, affording the Washington Senators their only world championship.

While baseball was his passion, Gowdy had a greater sense of duty. He became the first major league player to enlist in the U.S. armed services for duty in World War I, serving in France, and at the age of 53 he volunteered for World War II and was commissioned a major in the army. Stallings, long since in the grave, was still right about his catcher, who remained a leader on many fields.

Rick Dempsey had just turned 20 when he first made it to the major leagues in 1969, but it would be nine years before he would become a team's regular catcher, finally getting that opportunity with the Baltimore Orioles in 1978. By that time, Dempsey had come to accept his shortcomings as a hitter and realized that most of his energies had to go into catching if he hoped to continue drawing a major league paycheck. Better than most, he understood what it meant to play a role, since both of his parents had been actors on the vaudeville circuit. Dempsey proved to be quite adept at handling pitchers, made strong and true throws to second base and was quick to go nose to nose with an umpire who squeezed the corners. As long as Dempsey excelled behind the plate, the Orioles didn't care what he did beside the plate with a bat in his hands.

That arrangement worked for both parties for nine years, during which Dempsey batted a mere .241 and hit 72 home runs. Yet he became a different hitter when the calendar turned to October and championships were for the taking. Dempsey was a career .296 hitter in league playoff series, and he batted .286 in the 1979 World Series. But nothing he had done in baseball — or would do by the time he retired at age 43 after 24 seasons — measured up to his achievement in the 1983 World Series against the Philadelphia Phillies.

The Orioles were on the final lap of a brilliant 17-year run in which they finished below second in the standings only twice and went to the Series five times. Baltimore's stars were Eddie Murray and young Cal Ripken, Jr., but it was Dempsey, a .231 hitter that season, who tore into the Phillies' pitching. In 13 at-bats, he had five hits — four doubles and a home run — for a .385 average. His home run and double in Game 5 helped the Orioles finish off the Phillies. Asked to explain his hitting prowess, Dempsey shrugged and said, "Anybody's bound to get hot once in 15 years."

Dempsey also did his usual good work behind the plate, handling a pitching staff that fashioned a 1.60 ERA and held Mike Schmidt to 1 hit in 20 at-bats, and throwing out Joe Morgan on two of his three stolen-base attempts.

The Series ended in Philadelphia, and late that night the Orioles' traveling party piled into buses for the triumphant return to Baltimore. All except Dempsey and his wife. They drove the new Pontiac Trans-Am he had won for being voted the Series' Most Valuable Player — a lowly catcher living the hero's life for a few glorious hours.

RICK Dempsey
1983 | BALTIMORE ORIOLES

A couple of million people in Cardinal Nation would grab for the 12-gauge in their pickup gun rack if someone had the audacity to tell them that Pepper Martin was an "unlikely hero." But the truth is, no one could have expected that it would be Martin that would turn the 1931 World Series into his personal highlight reel, given his status as a callow rookie, the only player new to the St. Louis Cardinals lineup that season. Martin would become a .298 hitter over his 13 seasons with the Cardinals, lead the National League in stolen bases three times and stoke the furnace of the famed Gashouse Gang of the mid 1930s. Yet it all paled in comparison to those first 10 days in October 1931 when the rookie center fielder all but single-handedly denied a world championship to what was probably Connie Mack's greatest Philadelphia Athletics team.

To understand the connection that Cardinals fans make with Cardinals players, one must accept that following St. Louis baseball is not a pastime; it's a way of life. Players must earn their way into this culture with unbridled passion, fire and respect for the game. Pepper Martin gained entry the first time he whacked a base hit and didn't stop at first, belly flopping into second just ahead of a hurried throw.

He played in that hell-bent style every day, never taking his foot off the gas, on and off the field. He dropped water balloons off balconies onto the heads of innocent bystanders, shot pigeons from his hotel room window, drove midget race cars. He hitchhiked to his first spring training because he had no other means to get there. He was maestro of the Mississippi Mudcats, a jug-and-washboard band in the Cardinals clubhouse. An unpretentious lad from the Oklahoma dust bowl, Martin wore blue jeans and work shirts, no socks and usually had grease under his fingernails from working on his midget racers. He was quite a character, and it all added to his charm, but at the root, Martin was a ballplayer's ballplayer, and for that he was among the cherished treasures of Cardinal Nation.

Martin was 27 before he finally fought his way into the Cardinals lineup, and he batted .300 that first season. The Cardinals were in the Series for the second year in a row. The A's, a juggernaut that featured Lefty Grove, Mickey Cochrane, Jimmie Foxx and Al Simmons, all destined for the Hall of Fame, were after their third successive world championship.

The Cardinals lost Game 1 to Grove, but Martin had three hits. A day later, his daring on the bases accounted for both runs in a 2-0 victory. He had two hits in each of the next two games, and then had three hits, including a home run, and four RBIs in a 5-1 victory that gave the Cardinals a 3-2 edge in victories. After the A's tied the Series, the Cardinals became world champions in Game 7 with a 4-2 victory, but not before Martin grabbed Max Bishop's sinking liner to center with two outs in the ninth and two A's on base.

Martin had 12 hits in the Series and batted .500. He scored five runs and drove in five, had four doubles and a home run. He stole five bases against Cochrane and probably would have made off with the great catcher's underwear, too, if it had been worth another base.

PEPPER Martin
1931 | ST. LOUIS CARDINALS

Bucky Dent had secured a permanent place in baseball lore before the 1978 World Series began. His improbable home run over Fenway Park's Green Monster on the day after the regular season was supposed to have ended pushed the New York Yankees to a victory over the Boston Red Sox that broke the first-place tie in the American League East. The Yankees, who had trailed Boston by 14 games in July, went to the playoffs while the Red Sox and their fans struggled with the dagger in their hearts and nodded in agreement as their manager, Don Zimmer, muttered over and over, "Bucky 'Fucking' Dent."

Dent was the Yankees shortstop, and he was a fine fit on this team. The Yankees had plenty of good hitters, so they could afford Dent's .247 career average down at the bottom of the batting order. He was in the lineup to field and throw, make the double play, keep the other team's outs to three per inning, and he was wholly dependable in all of those areas. The second baseman, Willie Randolph, was just as sure-handed as Dent and a much better offensive player. But Randolph got hurt late in the season, so Brian Doyle became Dent's double-play partner for most of the playoffs and World Series.

Doyle was a rookie who had played in only 39 games and batted .192 that season. Incredibly, that would be the high mark of his four years in the major leagues. Doyle, who was sent packing for good in 1981 with a .161 career average, is one of only 50 players in major league history with more than 200 plate appearances and a batting average lower than .180. A slightly built player, he was easily overpowered by pitchers who threw hard and was baffled by offerings that had a bend or a hook to them.

Had Dent and Doyle merely played steady defense against the Los Angeles Dodgers, the Yankees would have been forever grateful. Had one of them contributed a little something with his bat, that would have been a pleasant surprise. As it was, both Dent and Doyle had the greatest eight days of their professional lives that October as the Yankees won the Series in six games.

Reggie Jackson, "Mr. October," batted .391 with two homers and eight RBIs, and hardly anybody noticed. That's because Doyle pounded away at a .438 clip, going 7 for 16 and scoring four runs. Dent had 10 hits, seven RBIs, and a .417 average. In the decisive Game 6, Dent had three hits and three RBIs, and Doyle had three hits and two RBIs in the Yankees' 7-2 victory. It was an extraordinary time for two players who just as quickly ducked back into the shadows of obscurity.

Series heroes Brian Doyle and Bucky Dent started a double play at second base in Game 6. Dent leaped to avoid Bill Russell.

BRIAN Doyle & BUCKY Dent

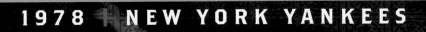

1978 | NEW YORK YANKEES

BILLY Martin

1953 | NEW YORK YANKEES

Hank Bauer scored the winning run in Game 6, driven home by Billy Martin's single, and the Yankees celebrated their fifth consecutive world championship.

Billy Martin was not a man welcome in polite company. He could be loud, boisterous, and crude — and some said those were the best of his civil qualities. Yet throughout his life, Martin was always welcome on a ballfield, largely because of his grit and spirit that greatly transcended his otherwise modest skills. Martin, as the cliché goes, rose to the occasion. If there was a rally in the making — or trouble to get into — he was usually in the thick of things. In grudging praise, Cleveland Indians general manager Frank Lane once said of Martin, "He's the kind of guy you'd like to kill if he's playing for the other team — but you'd like 10 of him on your side."

Martin played second base for the New York Yankees in seven seasons in the 1950s, his brash and aggressive style winning favor from manager Casey Stengel while enraging opponents, who nicknamed him "The Brat." Martin played in the World Series in five of those seasons, and it was on the big stage that he had his grandest moments as a player. In 28 Series games, Martin — a career .257 hitter with minimal power — batted .333 with five home runs and 19 RBIs.

In Game 7 of the 1952 Series, the Brooklyn Dodgers had the bases loaded with two outs in the seventh inning. Jackie Robinson lifted a pop-up to the right side that drifted in the wind and was about to fall safely. Martin dashed in and made a lunging catch at his shoetops, preserving a 4-2 lead and a Yankees' victory.

The same teams were in the Series a year later, and Martin was at his all-time best as the Yankees won in six games. This was a Yankees team that had powerful hitters named Mickey Mantle, Yogi Berra, Gene Woodling and Hank Bauer in their lineup. Yet it was the scrappy second baseman Martin who tore the Dodgers apart, batting .500, driving in 8 runs and knocking out 12 hits, a record for a six-game Series.

Martin's final hit in the 1953 Series came in dramatic fashion. Carl Furillo's two-run homer had tied the score for Brooklyn in the top of the ninth inning of Game 6 at Yankee Stadium. In their turn at bat, the Yankees put two runners on base. Martin shot a single to center field. As Martin rounded first base, Bauer scored, giving the Yankees a 4-3 victory for their fifth consecutive world championship.

Gene Tenace was a .241 hitter for his 15 seasons in the major leagues, yet for a period in 1977 he was the fourth-richest player in the game by virtue of his five-year, $1.8 million contract with the San Diego Padres. How was a .241 hitter able to climb into the high-rent district usually reserved for superstars? Simple — by earning a reputation as a player whose value far transcended his batting average.

GENE Tenace

1972 | OAKLAND ATHLETICS

Tenace had such a discerning batting eye that six times he drew more than 100 walks in a season, twice leading his league. His career on-base percentage of .391 was more reminiscent of a leadoff batter than a slew-footed catcher/first baseman who usually batted sixth or seventh in the lineup.

Tenace got more production from his hits than any other player of his era. In 1974, for example, he scored 71 runs and drove in 73, phenomenal totals for a player who batted .211. He did it by sending 44 of his 102 hits for extra bases, including 26 home runs (Tenace's 58 singles that season are the fewest ever by a player who appeared in 150 or more games) and walking a league-leading 110 times.

Tenace got to the major leagues in 1969 with the Oakland Athletics, and it took a few years for the team to recognize his subtle skills. He was a reserve until the late stages of the 1972 season, but as catcher Dave Duncan's batting average plummeted ever closer to .200, manager Dick Williams began using Tenace more frequently. By the time the American League playoffs rolled around, Tenace had taken Duncan's job. It was perhaps the most timely lineup change in baseball history, given what was about to happen.

Tenace was 0 for 16 in the playoffs until driving home a run with a single in Game 5 that gave the A's a 2-1 victory over Detroit and the pennant. Oakland moved on to the World Series against the Cincinnati Reds, but they were without their best player, Reggie Jackson, who had a disabling hamstring injury. There would be six one-run games in the seven-game Series, and three of them would be decided by Tenace. In Game 1, he became the first player to hit home runs in his first two Series at-bats, driving in all the A's runs in a 3-2 victory. In Game 4, he hit a home run in the fifth inning and had a single in a two-run rally in the ninth inning that gave the A's another 3-2 win. In Game 7, Tenace drove in two runs in the A's third 3-2 victory.

For the Series, Tenace batted .348, hit four home runs — one fewer than he had during the regular season — and drove home nine of the A's 16 runs; no other A's player had more than one RBI. The following two seasons, he was the regular first baseman on A's teams that repeated as world champions.

Gene Tenace's run-scoring single gave the A's a 2-1 victory in the decisive game of the American League Championship Series. The catcher was Bill Freehan, and the umpire was Nestor Chylak.

BOBBY Richardson

1960 | NEW YORK YANKEES

If good intentions and clean living were the keys to baseball success, Bobby Richardson would be the greatest second baseman in history. He became a Christian as a teenager and never wavered in his spiritual conviction during a 12-year career with the New York Yankees, despite temptation sitting on just about every other stool in the clubhouse. The Yankees of the 1950s and 1960s had a reputation for living the high life and burning the candle at both ends, yet most were fast friends with Richardson and held enormous respect for him, even if they couldn't quite understand why a fellow who lived such an exemplary life couldn't hit any better than he did. "Look at him — he doesn't drink, he doesn't smoke, he doesn't chew, he doesn't stay out late and he still can't hit .250!" an exasperated Casey Stengel, Richardson's first manager, once said. When it came time to square accounts at the end, many of Richardson's contemporaries summoned him for help. He led services at the funerals of Mickey Mantle, Roger Maris, Enos Slaughter and Dick Howser, among others.

Do not, however, get the idea that Richardson was more missionary than ballplayer. During his eight seasons playing regularly for the Yankees, he supplanted Nellie Fox as the best second baseman in the American League. A sure-handed fielder and very quick on the double play whether making the pivot or feeding the ball to shortstop Tony Kubek, Richardson won five consecutive Gold Glove awards. But Yankees never knew what to expect from Richardson as a hitter — his batting average ranged from .247 to .302 in his years as a regular. He took a heavy bat to the plate and swung as hard as he could, not the traditional approach for a man who is five-foot-nine, 170 pounds, and that was the best explanation for his inconsistencies.

Richardson was true to form in the World Series, playing in five of them during his years as a regular and batting anywhere from .391 to .148. He was at his greatest in the 1960 Series against the Pittsburgh Pirates. In the seven games, Richardson had 11 hits, including a grand slam and two triples, batted .367 and scored eight runs. His 12 RBIs — he had only 26 in 150 games during the season — set a Series record, as did his six RBIs in one game. Yet Richardson wasn't even the most famous second baseman in that Series. He was nudged out of glory's blaze by Bill Mazeroski, who knocked one over the left-field wall at Forbes Field in the bottom of the ninth in Game 7 — the only Game 7 that has ever ended with a home run. Though it provided little consolation for him, Richardson was voted the Most Valuable Player of the 1960 Series. It was the only time a player from the losing team has received the award.

Bobby Richardson displayed his bat that accounted for six RBIs in Game 3. Gil McDougald, Elston Howard and Bill Skowron greeted Richardson after his grand slam in the first inning.

Al Weis lasted 10 seasons in Major League Baseball, an extraordinary achievement for someone who batted .219, hit seven home runs and had a .279 on-base percentage. The average player of that period was a .253 hitter and had a .319 on-base percentage. Weis managed to hang around for a decade because he was a capable fielder at three positions — second base, third base and shortstop. Good defensive players were especially important to Weis' second team, the New York Mets, which relied more on pitching than hitting, so he was always in good favor, no matter how poorly he hit.

About the only time Weis made a headline during his six seasons with the Chicago White Sox had been for a jarring collision with Baltimore's Frank Robinson in 1967. Weis came out of it okay; Robinson, probably the best player in the American League, suffered from double vision for a month and missed 28 games, crippling the Orioles' pennant chances.

Weis joined the Mets in 1968, the year the team started coming of age. Their 73-89 record was good for only ninth place in the 10-team National League, but it marked the first time the seven-year-old Mets had lost fewer than 90 games in a season.

The following summer, man walked on the moon and the Mets won the pennant — no one was certain which was the more unbelievable achievement. Weis played his usual role, batting .215, playing 52 games at shortstop, 43 at second base. In July, though, about the time Neil Armstrong was taking his historic steps off Apollo 11, Weis trekked over some unfamiliar ground of his own. In two consecutive games, he hit home runs that helped the Mets beat the league-leading Chicago Cubs.

Ken Boswell, a left-handed batter, had been the Mets' primary second baseman during the season, but it was Weis who got most of the work in the World Series because he batted right-handed, a more favorable matchup against left-handed pitchers Mike Cuellar and Dave McNally, who started four of the five games for the American League champion Orioles. For reasons that no one was quite able to comprehend, Weis began to hit as if he were Pete Rose. He delivered a game-winning single in the ninth inning of Game 2 that afforded the Mets a 2-1 victory. In Game 5, he hit a seventh-inning home run off McNally at Shea Stadium that tied the score 3-3, after which the Mets finished off the Orioles and won the world championship. It was the only time in his career that Weis hit a home run in his home park. For the Series, he had five hits in 11 at-bats. His .455 batting average was the best on either team.

For the rest of his career, Weis couldn't even get back to being the old Al Weis. He batted just .189 in 132 at-bats before he retired during the 1971 season.

AL WEIS

1969 | NEW YORK METS

★★★★★★★★★★★★★★★★

1928
BABE RUTH, NEW YORK YANKEES

2002
BARRY BONDS, SAN FRANCISCO GIANTS

1932
LOU GEHRIG, NEW YORK YANKEES

1993
PAUL MOLITOR, TORONTO BLUE JAYS

1960
MICKEY MANTLE, NEW YORK YANKEES

1976
THURMAN MUNSON, NEW YORK YANKEES

1967
LOU BROCK, ST. LOUIS CARDINALS

1971
ROBERTO CLEMENTE, PITTSBURGH PIRATES

1970
BROOKS ROBINSON, BALTIMORE ORIOLES

★★★★★★★★★★★★★★★★

AN AMERICAN CLASSIC

GREAT HITTERS

WHO ROSE TO THE OCCASION

THE WORLD SERIES AT 100

There was nothing suspenseful about the 1928 World Series. The New York Yankees were in all their glory, and for the second consecutive season they demolished their National League opponent as swiftly as a tornado flattens a thatched hut. It was the St. Louis Cardinals' turn to keel over under the awesome might of the Yankees. New York used just three pitchers in the Series and outscored the Cardinals 27-10.

Babe Ruth

⫘ 1928 | NEW YORK YANKEES ⫘

This Series is noteworthy because it was the best ever for the great Babe Ruth, and he played in 10 of them. The Babe often got bored when the competition wasn't keen, but that was not the case in October 1928. In the four-game sweep, he had 10 hits in 16 at-bats for a .625 average, scored nine runs and had six extra-base hits, including three home runs in Game 4. Ruth's batting average, runs and extra-base hits set Series records that stood for more than 50 years.

Lou Gehrig also played magnificently, batting .545 with four home runs and nine RBIs, but —as usual — the Babe upstaged him.

Game 4 was at Sportsman's Park in St. Louis. In both the fourth and seventh innings, Ruth hit majestic drives that cleared the right-field roof. In the eighth,

41-year-old Pete Alexander, who was winding down a spectacular career, was pitching for the Cardinals when Ruth came to bat. Alexander, too, shot a glance over his left shoulder to watch in awe as Ruth's third home run of the day sailed over the right-field roof.

Ruth played left field that day and, with two outs in the bottom of the ninth and two runners on base, he ran to the fence and grabbed a fly ball that would otherwise have gone for a home run.

All in all, it was another incredible year for the Yankees and Ruth. Their only setback came that November when Herbert Hoover, the Republican presidential candidate, defeated Al Smith. Ruth and his teammates had publicly backed the Democrat.

CAREER LEADERS
HOME RUNS

	No.	WS	G		No.	WS	G
MICKEY MANTLE	18	12	65	DUKE SNIDER	11	6	36
BABE RUTH	15	10	41	LOU GEHRIG	10	7	34
YOGI BERRA	12	14	75	REGGIE JACKSON	10	5	27

Babe Ruth crossed home plate after hitting the first of his three home runs in Game 4 in 1928. Lou Gehrig waited to greet the Babe. The catcher was Earl Smith, and the umpire was Cy Pfirman.

Barry Bonds

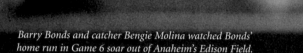

2002 | SAN FRANCISCO GIANTS

Over the course of three seasons, Barry Bonds had separated himself from the pack. Major League Baseball had its superstars, and he had been in that group. But with his achievements in 2000, 2001 and 2002, he had gone to a level beyond, as Michael Jordan had once done in basketball. In that span, Bonds set the season home run record, won his first batting title with a .370 average in a year in which the league norm was .255, set the season records for walks and on-base percentage and hit 27 percent of his 613 career home runs. He was in his late 30s, and he had come to master baseball like few, if any, before him; he had become a god among mortals on the ballfield.

Barry Bonds and catcher Bengie Molina watched Bonds' home run in Game 6 soar out of Anaheim's Edison Field.

But there was a darkness to his record that Bonds longed to brighten. He had been a meager performer in postseason play, blamed on five occasions for his team's failure to advance. In three National League Championship Series with the Pittsburgh Pirates in the early 1990s, and in division playoff series with the San Francisco Giants in 1997 and 2000, Bonds might as well have been Mario Mendoza. In 27 games, he batted only .196 with one home run and six RBIs.

The Giants afforded Bonds another chance for postseason glory in 2002, his 17th season. Even though he glared disdainfully at anyone who dared suggest he had something to prove, he certainly performed as if his legacy were at stake. In two playoff series, he reached base in 22 of 42 plate appearances, batted .286, hit four home runs, scored 10 runs and drove in 10 runs. Then it was on to his first World Series. He made his defining statement in his first at-bat, cracking a home run deep into the night. By the time the Series was over, he had reached base in 21 of 30 plate appearance, batted .471, hit four home runs, drove in six runs and walked a record 13 times.

The Anaheim Angels were so fearful that Bonds alone might be able to beat them that only 39 of their 112 pitches to him were strikes. The Angels, though, won Game 6 after trailing 5-0, and a day later they took the Series. Bonds had excelled, but it was not enough. He was sorely disappointed, but it had been the most satisfying journey of his career. "I'm not going to lie — it was fun; it was great," he said.

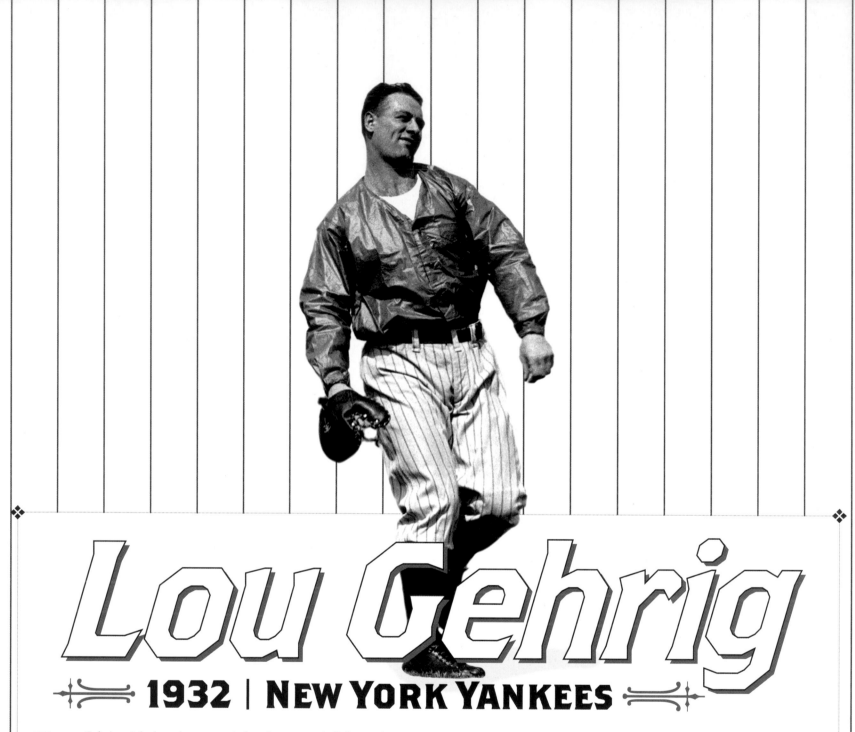

Lou Gehrig

1932 | NEW YORK YANKEES

L ou Gehrig might have been regarded as the greatest ballplayer who ever lived, except that he played on the same team as Babe Ruth, who cast the longest shadow ever on any field of play. Ruth's achievement was so extraordinary that he seemed a god among mortals, but when the spotlight occasionally widened to make room for someone else, it was usually Gehrig who was crowding the Babe. Once asked about having such an oversize character as a teammate and a rival for glory, the ever-modest Gehrig said, "It's a pretty big shadow. It gives me lots of room to spread myself."

Gehrig was at his greatest in the New York Yankees' four-game sweep of the Chicago Cubs in the 1932 World Series, but even then Ruth's "called shot" upstaged

his brilliance. The home run was Ruth's second of the game. Gehrig also hit two home runs that day, the second shortly after Ruth circled the bases on his "called shot." When the Yankees finished off the Cubs the following day, Ruth had just one hit in five at-bats, while Gehrig went 2 for 4 with three RBIs in a 13-6 victory.

Gehrig's work for the Series was truly impressive — 9 for 17 for a .529 average, three home runs, nine runs scored and eight RBIs — yet all anyone wanted to know from the Iron Horse was whether he saw Ruth point to the bleachers from his vantage point in the on-deck circle. Ever the good sport, Gehrig said, "What do you think of the nerve of that big monkey calling his shot and getting away with it?" furthering a legend that forever encroached on his own.

Paul Molitor

Paul Molitor was one of the most brittle players in the major leagues during his 15 seasons with the Milwaukee Brewers, missing more than 500 games because of injury and serving 10 terms on the disabled list. He was an exceptional athlete, highly capable at any of the infield positions and a quick and fast runner who stole more than 500 bases during his career — but the man just kept getting hurt.

Then he joined the Toronto Blue Jays in 1993 at age 36 and became a paragon of health. The Blue Jays had the good sense to keep Molitor off the field by employing him almost exclusively as their designated hitter. In his three seasons with the Blue Jays, Molitor played in 96 percent of the team's games and accounted for 508 of its hits, a stretch of productivity that went a long way toward his career count of 3,319 hits, eighth most in history.

The early 1990s were the Blue Jays' salad days. Skydome, billed as the world's most advanced and luxurious stadium, opened in 1989, and most of its 50,500 seats were filled for every game for the next five years. The team was a perennial contender in the American League East, won the World Series in 1992 and was back again in 1993, this time with Molitor as their DH. He had achieved perhaps his finest season, batting .332 and setting career highs with 22 home runs and 111 RBIs. He was even

CAREER LEADERS
BATTING AVERAGE

	AVG.	H	AB	WS	G
PEPPER MARTIN	.418	23	55	3	15
PAUL MOLITOR	.418	23	55	2	13
LOU BROCK	.391	34	87	3	21
MARQUIS GRISSOM	.390	30	77	3	19
THURMAN MUNSON	.373	25	67	3	16

MINIMUM 50 AT-BATS

better in the Series, as the Blue Jays beat the Philadelphia Phillies in six games.

This was not virgin ground for Molitor; in 1982 with the Brewers, he became the first player to get five hits in a Series game. Eleven years later, Molitor had 12 hits in 24 at-bats, including two doubles, two triples and two home runs. He drove in eight runs and tied a Series record by scoring 10 times.

Few players have ever performed so brilliantly on baseball's biggest stage, but Molitor would be a bit player in the end. In the bottom of the ninth inning of Game 6, he reached base with a single, after Rickey Henderson had drawn a walk. Joe Carter then cranked a home run into the left-field seats that provided the Blue Jays with an 8-6 victory and brought the Series to a stunning end. It was only fitting that Molitor scored the decisive run. He had earned a world championship ring, the only one of his 21-year career.

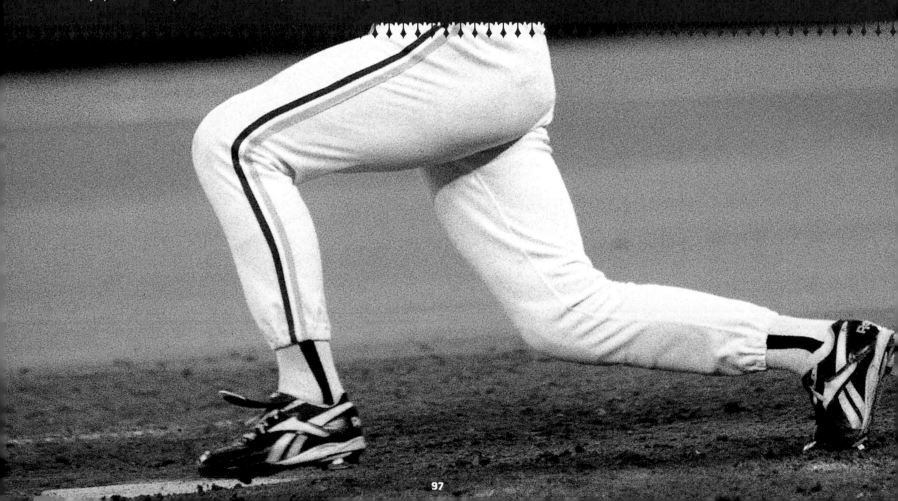

Mickey Mantle connected for one of his two home runs in Game 2. The catcher was Smoky Burgess, and the umpire was Johnny Stevens.

It must have been something to be there when Mickey Mantle was a kid on a bullet to the New York Yankees. Listen to someone who was, the long-forgotten outfielder Jack Reed:

"The first time I saw Mickey, I said, 'Good night, ol' Moses! — there is one fine-lookin' ballplayer.' He was so young, so strong, and he looked immaculate in that white Yankee uniform, like he was born to wear it. It seemed like he could run as fast as he wanted. Matter of fact, he could do almost anything he wanted."

Mickey Mantle

✦ 1960 | NEW YORK YANKEES ✦

Mantle became one of the great power hitters in history, limited only by his human frailties, of which there were many. He is the greatest slugger in World Series history, the all-time leader in home runs, RBIs, extra-base hits, total bases and walks. In 12 Series, he hit 18 home runs, three more than Babe Ruth, number two on the list. Reggie Jackson, who is called "Mr. October," hit just 10. It can be argued that Mantle should hold those records, given that he played in more Series games than anyone except Yogi Berra — but that would confuse playing with achieving, and Mantle did both. He was at his best in the 1960 Series against the Pittsburgh Pirates. The irony is that it also was his most crushing disappointment in baseball.

The Yankees demolished the Pirates in virtually every measurable category. They batted a Series-record .338 and held a 55-27 edge in runs. Mantle went 0 for 7 in Games 1, 4 and 5 — all Yankees losses. In the other four games, he went 10 for 18, hit three home runs, scored eight runs and drove in 11 runs — incredible totals even for a star of his magnitude.

In the top of the ninth inning of Game 7, his single scored one runner to cut the Yankees' deficit to 9-8 and sent another runner to third base. With one out, Berra slapped a hard grounder toward first base. Rocky Nelson grabbed the ball and stepped on first for an out, then spun toward second, anticipating a double play that would end the Series. But the alert Mantle had reversed his course and dove back into first before the startled Nelson could tag him, and the man on third sneaked home with the tying run.

So it was actually Mantle who afforded Bill Mazeroski the opportunity to hit the only home run that has ever ended Game 7 of the World Series. Mantle watched in dismay from center field as Mazeroski's drive disappeared over the left-field wall at Forbes Field in the bottom of the ninth, then dropped his head and sprinted to the clubhouse. Reporters found him at his locker, head bowed and weeping softly. His greatest Series was over, and it had not been enough.

CAREER LEADERS
RBIs

	No.	WS	G		No.	WS	G
MICKEY MANTLE	40	12	65	BABE RUTH	33	10	41
YOGI BERRA	39	14	75	JOE DiMAGGIO	30	10	51
LOU GEHRIG	35	7	34	BILL SKOWRON	29	8	39

Mantle had four hits in Game 3, including this home run in the fourth inning.

Thurman Munson

Thurman Munson slid past Johnny Bench and scored in the first inning of Game 4.

Thurman Munson was the captain of the New York Yankees in the mid 1970s when the team returned to glory. The greatest Yankees took on a regal look when they wore the famed pinstripes, but the uniform did little to enhance "Squatty Body," as Munson's teammates affectionately called him. Nonetheless, he was an exemplary ballplayer, a dependable hitter and a gritty catcher, a fierce and unyielding competitor. Babe Ruth, Joe DiMaggio and Mickey Mantle had not been honored with the title of captain. Munson was the Yankees' first captain since Lou Gehrig in the 1930s.

Munson and the Yankees found success together. In 1976, the team won its first American League pennant in 12 years, and Munson was selected the league's Most Valuable Player. He had a .302 batting average with 17 home runs and 105 RBIs during the season, and he batted .435 in the League Championship Series. But the World Series proved to be embarrassing and humiliating for the Yankees.

The Cincinnati Reds, the mighty Big Red Machine, rolled over New York in four games by a combined score of 22-8. Many things went wrong for the Yankees, but in the midst of the carnage, there stood Munson, battling until the bitter end. He had a hit in each of his last six at-bats and finished the Series with a .529 average, the highest ever for a player on the losing team; the rest of the Yankees batted .178.

The Series would prove to be a bittersweet experience for Munson in more ways than one. He always wanted to be the best at what he did, and this had been his chance to measure himself against the Reds' Johnny Bench, who by that time was being hailed as the best catcher in history. Bench hit two home runs and drove in five runs in the Reds' 7-2 victory in Game 5 and finished the Series with a .533 average. In the media briefing afterward, someone mentioned Munson and Bench in the same sentence to Reds manager Sparky Anderson. "Don't embarrass any catcher by comparing him with Johnny Bench," Anderson said sternly.

Munson was in the room, and Anderson's words seared his ears, but the proud catcher stuck out his jaw and held his head high. Unlike Anderson, Bench and the Reds, Munson would be back. The Yankees and their captain won the next two world championships.

Lou Brock

1967 | ST. LOUIS CARDINALS

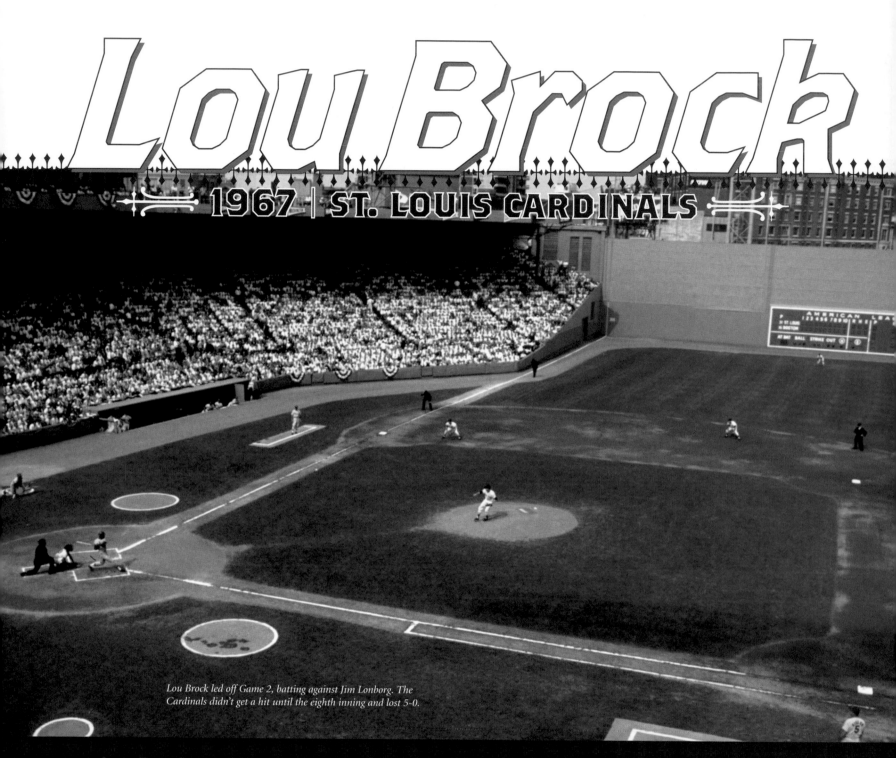

Lou Brock led off Game 2, batting against Jim Lonborg. The Cardinals didn't get a hit until the eighth inning and lost 5-0.

Lou Brock remains a symbol of the Chicago Cubs' futility. He was just a kid trying to find his way in the major leagues when the Cubs traded him to the St. Louis Cardinals in a June 1964 exchange that sent pitcher Ernie Broglio, an 18-game winner the previous season, to Chicago.

Broglio soon flamed out, going 7-19 before leaving baseball in 1966. Brock bloomed into a Hall of Fame player with the Cardinals. He broke Ty Cobb's all-time record for stolen bases, set the National League record for steals in a season and played in three World Series, which was three more than the Cubs had played in since 1945.

Brock didn't just play in three Series — he became one of the greatest performers in Series history. His .391 batting average is the highest among those who played in at least 20 Series games, and he shares the all-time record for stolen bases with 14.

Brock was at his best in the 1967 Series against the Boston Red Sox. It was "The Impossible Dream" season for the Red Sox, who had finished a half game out of last place the previous year. The Series was expected to be hotly contested, and it was. Ill will fueled the competition. One Boston newspaper wrote, "Take Bob Gibson out of the Cardinals' lineup, and you've got a loser." Red Sox manager Dick Williams, asked about his Game 7 plans, retorted, "Lonborg and cham-

pagne." The players' wives even got into it, accusing each other of hogging seats in the stands by draping mink coats over chair backs.

Brock had fashioned a magnificent season, batting .299 in a year when the league average was .249, leading the league in runs and stolen bases, and providing 21 home runs and 76 RBIs from his leadoff position in the batting order. The Cardinals' other great players, Orlando Cepeda, Tim McCarver and Roger Maris, finished the season poorly, and Cepeda and McCarver did not help much in the Series. Brock more than covered for his teammates' deficiencies. He batted .414, reached base 14 times in the seven games, scored eight runs and set a Series record with seven stolen bases. His final two hits came in Game 7, when Gibson out-pitched Jim Lonborg in a 7-2 Cardinals' triumph.

The Cardinals were in the Series again a year later. They lost to the Detroit Tigers in seven games, but not for lack of accomplishment on Brock's part. He batted .464 and had two home runs and seven stolen bases in what would his last appearance on baseball's biggest stage.

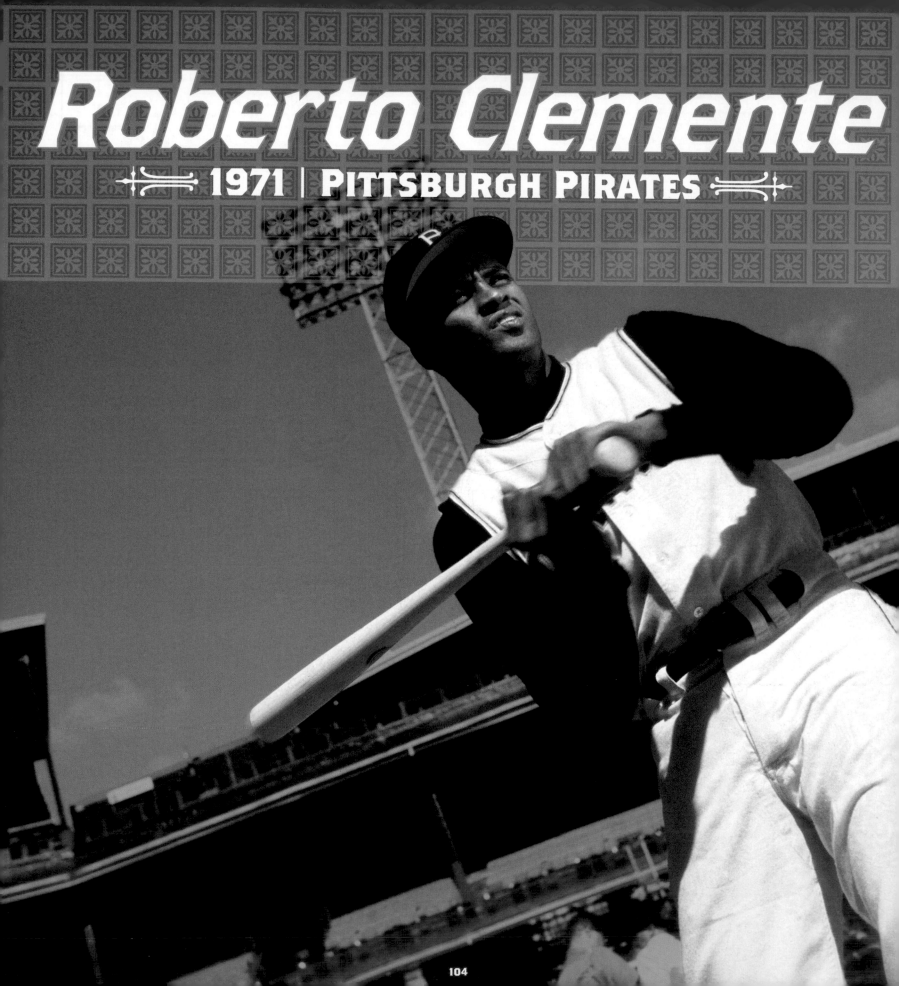

Roberto Clemente
✣ 1971 | PITTSBURGH PIRATES ✣

Before there was cable television, superstations, SportsCenter, athletic shoe endorsement deals and mlb.com, it was possible for a gifted ballplayer outside of New York to go underappreciated for his talents.

Such was the case with Roberto Clemente, a slashing hitter and elegant right fielder who spent the entirety of his 18 Major League Baseball seasons with the small-market Pittsburgh Pirates. Fans read about the feats of the great Clemente, and they could sometimes watch him in person if they had the means to visit a National League park, but for the most part he was the secret treasure of the denizens of Forbes Field and, later, Three Rivers Stadium.

It took a national stage and television coverage for Clemente to gain true recognition, and even then, the performer had to rise above the rest of the cast. Clemente batted .310 in the 1960 World Series against the New York Yankees, yet the face on that Fall Classic belongs (rightfully) to Bill Mazeroski. It would be 11 years before the Pirates would again be National League champions. Clemente was 37 years old by that time, yet he remained a formidable player, having batted .341 with 86 RBIs that season, playing a secondary role on his team only to Willie "Pops" Stargell and his 48 homers and 125 RBIs.

Pittsburgh's opponent in the World Series was the juggernaut from Baltimore, a team that had won more than 100 games for the third successive season. On the eve of the Series, Clemente was quietly resolute. "Now they will see how I play," he said firmly, referring to the world's baseball viewers.

Indeed, they did. In the seven games, Clemente had 12 hits in 29 at-bats for a .414 average, including two home runs, two doubles and a triple. He scored three runs and had four RBIs. He also had an opportunity to display his fabled right arm, a hose so strong that he led National League outfielders in assists a record five times. In Game 6, Baltimore's Frank Robinson struck a 300-foot fly ball toward Clemente, who made the catch and then unleashed a laser beam–like throw to the catcher. Merv Rettenmund, who was on third base and expected to tag up and score after the catch, stopped in his tracks and retreated to the bag. In Game 7, Clemente's home run afforded Pittsburgh a 1-0 lead in what would become a 2-1 Pirates' triumph. After accepting the trophy that went to the Most Valuable Player of the Series, Clemente said, "I want everybody in the world to know that this is the way I play all the time. All season, every season."

He would play just one more year. On the final day of the 1972 season, Clemente became the 11th player to achieve 3,000 hits for his career. Three months later he was dead, one of the victims on an overloaded DC-7 that crashed into the Caribbean Sea carrying him and others to Nicaragua with rescue supplies for earthquake victims.

Roberto Clemente watched the flight of his fourth-inning home run that gave the Pirates a 1-0 lead in Game 7.

Brooks Robinson

1970 | BALTIMORE ORIOLES

Three of Brooks Robinson's nine hits in the 1970 Series: a home run in Game 1, and a home run and a single in Game 4.

Brooks Robinson had just made another spectacular defensive play during the 1970 World Series, eliciting more gaping awe and disbelief on the Cincinnati Reds' side of the field. "Where do they plug that Hoover in?" groused Lee May, one of the hitters whom Robinson had robbed twice of hits.

Robinson was indeed a human vacuum cleaner at third base for the Baltimore Orioles, sucking up virtually everything that was hit his way. But this was nothing out of the ordinary. Fans in Baltimore and other American League locales had been treated for years to Robinson's wizardry. He is not the best third baseman in history — his .267 batting average and 268 home runs in 23 seasons don't measure up to others — but Robinson is universally regarded as the best fielder ever at his position. Or maybe Frank Robinson, a teammate of Brooks in Baltimore, had it right: "He was the best defensive player at *any* position. I used to stand in the outfield like a fan and watch him make play after play. I used to think, *Wow! I can't believe this.*"

Brooks Robinson was not a gifted athlete. He was slow afoot, and his body was more lumps than chiseled stone. But nobody had quicker reactions. "Worst athlete I ever saw," Jim Palmer, Baltimore's ace pitcher for many years, was fond of saying. Palmer would put a hand at his waist and lower it to his feet and say, "But I never saw a better athlete from here to here."

Robinson expected to be busier than usual during the 1970 Series, given that most of Cincinnati's regulars were right-handed hitters and two of Baltimore's top starting pitchers, Mike Cuellar and Dave McNally, were soft-tossing lefthanders. In Game 1, May ripped a shot down the third-base line that Robinson plucked beyond the bag in foul territory. He then spun and pegged a one-hopper to first that beat May. In Game 2, Robinson lunged for a smash by May, made a backhanded catch and started a double play. He made four spectacular plays in Game 3, two of them robbing Johnny Bench of hits and one resulting in a double play. When the Orioles finished off the Reds in Game 5, Robinson again frustrated Bench, grabbing his ninth-inning line drive that was hell-bent for left field.

All the while, Robinson was killing the Reds with his bat, too. He hit two home runs and two doubles, drove in six runs, and had a .429 batting average. When it was over and the Reds were collecting their thoughts, Bench spoke for the whole team. "I hope we can come back and play the Orioles next year," said the Reds catcher, who one day would join Robinson in the Hall of Fame. "I also hope Brooks Robinson has retired by then."

★ ★ ★ ★ ★ ★ ★ ★ ★ ★ ★ ★ ★ ★ ★ ★

1905
CHRISTY MATHEWSON, NEW YORK GIANTS

1967
BOB GIBSON, ST. LOUIS CARDINALS

1916
BABE RUTH, BOSTON RED SOX

1965
LOS ANGELES DODGERS STAFF

1926
PETE ALEXANDER, ST. LOUIS CARDINALS

1966
BALTIMORE ORIOLES STAFF

1937
LEFTY GOMEZ, NEW YORK YANKEES

1963
SANDY KOUFAX, LOS ANGELES DODGERS

1957
LEW BURDETTE, MILWAUKEE BRAVES

1961
WHITEY FORD, NEW YORK YANKEES

★ ★ ★ ★ ★ ★ ★ ★ ★ ★ ★ ★ ★ ★ ★ ★

AN AMERICAN CLASSIC

GREAT PITCHERS

WHO ROSE TO THE OCCASION

THE WORLD SERIES AT 100

CHRISTY
MATHEWSON

1905 | NEW YORK GIANTS

By most accounts, Christy Mathewson was the most admired and popular ballplayer of the early 20th century, before Babe Ruth came along.

Mathewson was the star pitcher of the New York Giants, the most famous team of the day, and his only equal was the Washington Senators' Walter Johnson. (Johnson ranks second and Mathewson is tied for third on the all-time list for victories.) Unlike most of his contemporaries, Mathewson had a college education and a genteel manner. He rarely smoked, drank or swore, and he refused to play ball on Sunday because he had promised his mother that he wouldn't. He was the pet of Giants manager John McGraw, who was crestfallen when he caught Mathewson playing dice with teammates one day. McGraw fined everyone $10 except Mathewson, who had to pay $100 because "you should have set a better example for these men who don't have your intelligence," McGraw said.

MOST WORLD SERIES SHUTOUTS

PITCHER	TIME PERIOD	NO.
CHRISTY MATHEWSON NEW YORK GIANTS	1905–1913	4
THREE FINGER BROWN CHICAGO CUBS	1906–1908	3
WHITEY FORD NEW YORK YANKEES	1960–1961	3
BILL DINEEN BOSTON RED SOX	1903	2
ART NEHF NEW YORK GIANTS	1921–1923	2
BILL HALLAHAN ST. LOUIS CARDINALS	1930–1931	2
ALLIE REYNOLDS NEW YORK YANKEES	1949–1952	2
LEW BURDETTE MILWAUKEE BRAVES	1957	2
SANDY KOUFAX LOS ANGELES DODGERS	1965	2

The Giants won the National League pennant in 1904, but McGraw refused to play in the World Series, which had been born a year earlier. He claimed the four-year-old American League was too inferior to be taken seriously. More likely, he feared that the Giants might be faced with playing the new team in town, the Highlanders (who would come to be known as the Yankees), and he didn't want to risk the embarrassment of losing.

The Giants won again a year later. This time McGraw agreed to play the AL champion, the Philadelphia Athletics. He fueled the fire by sending the Giants onto the field in black uniforms with WORLD'S CHAMPIONS stitched across the front. They would be the champions, once the 25-year-old Mathewson got done with the A's. He went to the mound in Game 1, Game 3 and the decisive Game 5, and each time he pitched a shutout — the only time that has ever been done in the Series. Mathewson won by scores of 3-0, 9-0 and 2-0 over a six-day period. In 27 innings, he gave up 14 hits, walked one and struck out 18.

Joe McGinnity also pitched a shutout for the Giants. The A's only victory was a shutout by Chief Bender. It was the only Series in which every game was decided by a shutout.

BOB GIBSON

1967 | ST. LOUIS CARDINALS

Bob Gibson and Jose Santiago, the starting pitchers for Game [...]
posed for photographers a day before the Series began.
OPPOSITE PAGE: *Gibson dominated the Red Sox in Game 4,*
pitching a five-hit shutout.

Whether Bob Gibson was the meanest pitcher who ever lived is beside the point. Perception is everything, and batters of his era believed that Gibson got just as much satisfaction from buzzing them inside and setting them on their keisters as he did from getting them out. "Bob wasn't unfriendly when he pitched — I'd say it was more like hateful," said Joe Torre, a St. Louis Cardinals teammate of Gibson's for six seasons. There was no finesse to Gibson's pitches; they all sped toward their target with unabated fury. He had two fastballs, one that sizzled in high, another that burrowed in low. His slider had a vicious break, and his curve was a bowel-locking pitch, the type that came straight at a batter and dipped and plummeted at the last second.

After Sandy Koufax retired in 1966, Gibson had a few years to himself as the most respected pitcher in the National League. In 1968, he had a 1.12 ERA and 13 shutouts, achievements that hadn't been seen since the dead ball era of the early 1900s. Batters hit only .184 against him in his 305 innings, and he came out of a game before the eighth inning only twice. During one stretch, he gave up two earned runs in 95 innings. He won 22 games. The most incredible part was that he lost nine, three because the Cardinals didn't score a run.

ONE-GAME STRIKEOUTS		
BOB GIBSON ST. LOUIS CARDINALS	1968	17
SANDY KOUFAX LOS ANGELES DODGERS	1963	15
CARL ERSKINE BROOKLYN DODGERS	1953	14
HOWARD EHMKE PHILADELPHIA PHILLIES	1929	13
BOB GIBSON ST. LOUIS CARDINALS	1964	13

Great as Gibson was from April to September, he was even better in his three World Series. He started nine games, won seven, completed all but one, struck out 92 in 81 innings and fashioned a 1.89 ERA. Three of those victories came in the 1967 Series against the Boston Red Sox, the "Impossible Dream" team. Gibson had missed two months after a line drive by Roberto Clemente smashed into him and broke his leg, but he was ready for the Series. Pitching at hostile Fenway Park in Game 1, he struck out 10 in a 2-1 victory. In Game 4, he pitched a five-hit shutout to give the Cardinals a 3-1 Series advantage.

The gritty Red Sox won the next two, and they were at home for Game 7, only Gibson standing in the way of their first world championship since 1918. He was pitching on three days' rest for only the second time all year.

It was one of those afternoons that reminds us why baseball holds a tight grip on many. Gibson didn't give up a hit until the fifth inning, cracked a home run of his own and finished off Boston 7-2, yielding only three hits and striking out 10. He was tired and his elbow ached, and he was running on fumes for the final three or four innings. But nobody on the Cardinals side dared suggest that he let someone else finish. No way, said his catcher, Tim McCarver. Nobody was brave enough to fight Bob Gibson.

BABE
RUTH

1916 | BOSTON RED SOX

"Pitching just felt like the most natural thing in the world. Striking out batters was easy."

— Babe Ruth

CAREER LEADERS
ERA

	ERA	WS	G	IP
Jack Billingham	0.36	3	11	25⅓
Harry Brecheen	0.83	3	3	32⅔
Babe Ruth	0.87	2	6	31
Sherry Smith	0.89	2	7	30⅓
Sandy Koufax	0.95	4	8	57
MIMIMUM 25 INNINGS				

Babe Ruth might have become the best left-handed pitcher in Major League Baseball history had he not started hitting home runs at a pace that suggested a higher calling.

A large man for the time, the six-foot-two, 200-pound Ruth cut an imposing figure on the pitcher's mound, and was said to have frightened batters. He threw a quick, darting fastball and a sharp-breaking curve. Unlike many pitchers of the day, he did not use a spitball or roughen the ball with an emery board or belt buckle to enhance its movement when thrown.

Ruth pitched full-time for the Boston Red Sox for three seasons beginning in 1915, and he continued to pitch on a part-time basis until 1919. By the age of 22, he had 67 wins. The top five left-handed winners of the 20th century — Warren Spahn, Steve Carlton, Eddie Plank, Lefty Grove and Tommy John — had a combined five wins by that age.

Ruth had some memorable pitching duels with the legendary Walter Johnson, posting a 6-3 record in their matchups, including three 1-0 victories. Asked how he had become such a good pitcher, Ruth said, "As soon as I got out there I felt a strange relationship with the pitcher's mound. It was as if I'd been born out there. Pitching just felt like the most natural thing in the world. Striking out batters was easy."

His pitching performances in the 1916 World Series and in the 1918 Series were stunning. Pitching Game 2 in 1916 against the Brooklyn Dodgers, Ruth gave up an inside-the-park home run in the first inning, then pitched 13 scoreless innings and earned a 2-1 victory. In the 1918 Series, he pitched a shutout against the Chicago Cubs in Game 1, and then in Game 4, he didn't give up any runs until the eighth inning. He had pitched 29⅔ consecutive scoreless innings, a Series record that stood until Whitey Ford broke it in 1961. In his three Series games as a pitcher, Ruth had a 3-0 record and a 0.87 ERA.

One of Ruth's more astute teammates, Harry Hooper, had noticed that the Babe was also an excellent hitter. Hooper suggested to manager Ed Barrow that perhaps Ruth should play in the outfield when he wasn't pitching. The Babe was all for the idea; long before it became an ESPN ad line, he realized that "Chicks dig the long ball." When Tris Speaker, the legendary center fielder and a former teammate of Ruth's, heard what Ruth was doing, he shook his head sadly. "Ruth made a grave mistake giving up pitching," Speaker said. "Working once a week, he might have lasted a long time and become a great star."

DODGERS
STAFF
1965 | LOS ANGELES DODGERS

Game 1 of the 1965 World Series fell on Yom Kippur, the holiest day of the Jewish calendar. Sandy Koufax, who had won 26 games during the season and struck out more batters than any other pitcher in history, excused himself from work for religious obligations, leaving Don Drysdale to pitch for the Los Angeles Dodgers. This did not cause great consternation among Dodgers followers, because Drysdale had won 23 games, the third-highest total in the major leagues. Still, it was a ray of hope for the Minnesota Twins, who cuffed Drysdale around and got superb pitching from their starter, Mudcat Grant, in an 8-2 victory. Now full of confidence, the Twins beat Koufax 5-1 the following day. He gave up only one earned run in six innings, but the Dodgers hitters could do little against Jim Kaat.

The Twins had now beaten two pitchers who would make the Hall of Fame, and the Dodgers' hitters had lived down to their reputation: Their offense had scored fewer runs during the season than any other National League teams except the two four-year-old expansion teams, the Houston Astros and New York Mets. But the Dodgers' pitching staff was the best in the major leagues that season, largely because of three men who had combined for 64 victories, started 76 percent of the games and pitched

Claude Osteen

63 percent of the innings. Along with Koufax and Drysdale, the third man in the group was Claude Osteen, a slightly built lefthander with a Tennessee drawl who answered to "Gomer" because of his striking facial resemblance to the star of the popular TV series *Gomer Pyle*. Osteen would pitch in the major leagues for 18 years. His performance in Game 3 might have been the finest of his career, given the circumstances. He held the Twins to five hits and completed a 4-0 shutout.

The Dodgers were now back to Drysdale and Koufax, who didn't falter a second time. Drysdale pitched a five-hitter and won 7-2, and Koufax pitched a four-hitter and won 7-0. After the Twins beat Osteen and tied the Series, Dodgers manager Walter Alston sent Koufax to the mound for Game 7 on two days' rest instead of Drysdale, who had had three days' rest. Koufax sent the Twins away whimpering, giving up only three hits in a 2-0 victory, the third shutout of the Series for the Dodgers. Only one other team had done that; the 1905 New York Giants had four shutouts, three by the legendary Christy Mathewson. Koufax had given up one earned run and struck out 29 in 24 innings, but he might not have gotten three chances had Osteen not come through with the game of his life.

THE DODGERS' VICTORIES

			IP	H	R	ER	BB	SO
GAME 3	4-0	CLAUDE OSTEEN	9	5	0	0	2	2
GAME 4	7-2	DON DRYSDALE	9	5	2	2	2	11
GAME 5	7-0	SANDY KOUFAX	9	4	0	0	11	0
GAME 7	2-0	SANDY KOUFAX	9	3	0	0	3	10

Sandy Koufax and Don Drysdale celebrated after Koufax's National League pennant-clinching victory over the Milwaukee Braves in 1965.

PETE ALEXANDER

1926 | ST. LOUIS CARDINALS

Pete Alexander drank so heavily that the Chicago Cubs didn't know from one day to the next whether he would show up at all, and if he did, whether he would be in any condition to pitch. He not only drank enormous quantities of gin, but also rubbed it into his skin. The shock of it was that, even though Alexander was 39, ravaged by alcoholism, given to epileptic fits and partially deaf from the thunderous shellings he had experienced in World War I, the man still had incredible faculties on the pitcher's mound. Only a handful in Major League Baseball history can show achievement that doesn't pale in comparison to Alexander the Great's. He won 373 games (tied for third best all-time), had three successive 30-win seasons and nine 20-win seasons and pitched 16 shutouts in one season.

ABOVE: *Pete Alexander and Bob Shawkey, the starting pitchers in Game 6, exchanged pleasantries before going to work.* RIGHT: *Alexander and Jesse Haines each beat the Yankees twice and held them to six runs in 37 innings.*

Nonetheless, the exasperated Cubs fired Alexander during the 1926 season. He soon found work with the St. Louis Cardinals, who were bearing down on their first National League pennant. Alexander stayed sober enough to help the Cardinals along with nine victories. They were underdogs in the World Series against the New York Yankees, who had their famed "Murderers' Row" lineup in place for the first time that season. There was nothing, however, that could shake the redoubtable Alexander, who, as the old expression goes, had seen the elephant and heard the owl many times over.

He pitched complete-game victories in Game 2 and in Game 6, striking out a total of 16 Yankees. Here's where the legend gets fuzzy. Some claim that Alexander went on a major league bender after his Game 6 triumph and was sleeping it off in the bullpen as Game 7 wore into the late innings; others — mostly his relatives — swear that he returned to his hotel room after his win, sipped a glass of warm milk and slept like a baby. Whatever the case, the Cardinals were in the soup in the bottom of the seventh inning at Yankee Stadium. They led 3-2 and had two outs, but the bases were loaded and Tony Lazzeri, a .309 hitter with 102 RBIs during the season, was the next batter. Jesse Haines had torn open a blister on his pitching hand, the result of throwing one too many knuckleballs. Rogers Hornsby, the Cardinals' player/manager, signaled to the bullpen. Here's what James R. Harrison of *The New York Times* wrote the following day:

"Forty thousand pairs of eyes peered anxiously through the gray mist toward the bullpen out in deep left. There was a breathless pause, and then around the corner of the stand came a tall figure in a Cardinal sweater. His cap rode rakishly on the corner of his head. He walked like a man who was going nowhere in particular and was in no hurry to get there. He was a trifle knock-kneed and his gait was not a model of grace and rhythm. Any baseball fan would have known him from a mile away. It was Grover Cleveland ["Pete"] Alexander. Alexander the Great was coming in to pull the Cardinal machine out of the mudhole. The ancient twirler, who had gone nine full innings the day before, was shuffling in where younger men feared to tread."

Alexander got his man, striking out Lazzeri on a 2-2 curveball that bent under the hitter's flailing bat. The old master put away the Yankees in the eighth and retired two more in the ninth before he walked Babe Ruth. Ruth bolted for second base, and catcher Bob O'Farrell, after overcoming his surprise, threw out the Bambino trying to steal, for the final out of the Series. It was a grand signature on Alexander's brilliant, yet flawed, career. He had a few more good years in him, but his demons eventually got the best of him.

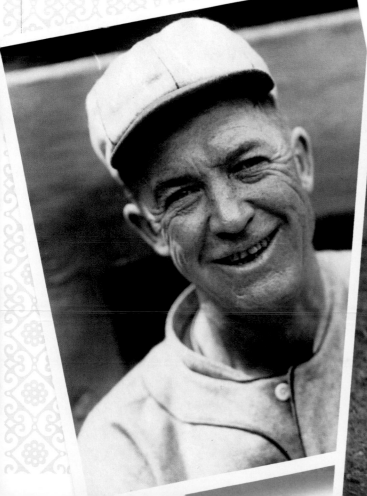

*Moe Drabowsky, Wally Bunker, Jim Palmer and Dave McNally celebrated the Orioles'
first world championship. The group held the Dodgers scoreless for the final 33 innings
of the four games.*

THE ORIOLES' VICTORIES

				IP	H	R	ER	BB	SO
GAME 1	5-2		DAVE MCNALLY	2 1/3	2	2	2	5	1
			MOE DRABOWSKY	6 2/3	1	0	0	2	11
GAME 2	1-0		JIM PALMER	9	4	0	0	3	6
GAME 3	1-0		WALLY BUNKER	9	6	0	0	1	6
GAME 4	1-0		DAVE MCNALLY	9	4	0	0	2	4

ORIOLES
STAFF
1966 | BALTIMORE ORIOLES

The Los Angeles Dodgers were coming to the end of an era in 1966, and the Baltimore Orioles were just coming of age. The Dodgers were in the World Series for the third time in four years, but within a few months Sandy Koufax would be forced into retirement because of an arthritic left elbow, and the team's already weak offense would lose two of its better players when Maury Wills and Tommy Davis were traded away.

The Orioles were in the Series for the first time since the franchise had moved from St. Louis in 1954. They were young and talented, and that year they had gotten Frank Robinson, as good a player as there was, in a trade with the foolish Cincinnati Reds. Within a few years, Earl Weaver would be the manager and all the pieces — 20-game winners, Gold Glove winners, Robinsons named Frank and Brooks — would be in place for a team that would win 318 games and three American League pennants from 1969 to 1971.

But in 1966, the Dodgers could still send Koufax, Don Drysdale and Claude Osteen out to pitch on successive days, and it didn't get any better than that. The Orioles' starting pitchers for the Series were 23-year-old Dave McNally, 20-year-old Jim Palmer and 21-year-old Wally Bunker. Palmer, especially, had exceptional ability, and a brashness that often crossed into arrogance. "You can beat the Dodgers with a fastball," he declared, an insult to even the weakest of major league hitters.

Whatever McNally was throwing to the Dodgers in Game 1 wasn't working well. He had a 4-0 lead to work with, but got in so much trouble in the third inning that Moe Drabowsky was summoned from the bullpen. The 31-year-old Drabowsky had once been a highly regarded commodity, but had had many arm problems. By this time, he was a well-traveled journeyman, working for his fifth team in 11 years. He was also a well-known practical joker, doing things like using the bullpen telephone to call Hong Kong restaurants and order moo shu pork to be delivered. Drabowsky was in rare form on this day, giving up no runs and only one hit in the final 6⅔ innings and striking out 11, including six in a row, in a 5-2 victory. Little did the Dodgers know when they scored two runs in the third inning that there would be no more for them for the year.

Palmer threw his fastballs in Game 2 and gained a 6-0 victory over Koufax, who was victimized by center fielder Willie Davis' three errors in the fifth inning. Bunker and McNally finished off the Dodgers with 1-0 shutouts in Games 3 and 4. Paul Blair hit a home run for Bunker, and Frank Robinson hit one for McNally.

The Dodgers went 33 innings without scoring and batted .142. Either it was the most inept Series hitting performance since the 1905 Philadelphia Athletics failed to score in four games, or it was the best pitching performance since the 1965 Dodgers shut out the Minnesota Twins three times.

Lefty Gomez was the funnyman of the great New York Yankees' teams of the 1930s. He was perhaps the only person who could needle Joe DiMaggio and get a toothy grin from the Yankee Clipper instead of the famous DiMaggio stare.

LEFTY GOMEZ

1937 | NEW YORK YANKEES

Gomez met a Broadway actress who would become his wife and invited her to watch him pitch. She had never been to a major league game before, and after Gomez lost, she told him, "Don't let it worry you; you'll beat 'em tomorrow."

"Tomorrow!" Gomez shrieked. "Who the hell do you think you're marrying — Iron Man McGinnity?"

During Game 2 of the 1936 World Series, Gomez paused on the mound to admire an airplane passing over the stadium, much to the chagrin of his manager, Joe McCarthy. "What are you doing out there, you nut? Trying to lose the game for us?" McCarthy roared. Poker-faced, Gomez replied, "Relax, skipper. I've never seen a pitcher lose a game by not throwing the ball."

In addition to comic relief, Gomez provided the Yankees with some of the best pitching in their history. Though he carried no more than 165 pounds on his 6-foot-2 frame, Gomez threw extremely hard and had a big, sweeping curveball that kept hitters lunging. Later, he changed to a finesse style because of persistent arm soreness, and continued to be effective. With Gomez and Red Ruffing — one of the greatest lefty/righty combinations in baseball history — at the top of the pitching rotation, the Yankees won pennants in 1932, 1936, 1937, 1938 and 1939. Gomez started seven games in those five World Series, and the Yankees won them all. He beat the New York Giants in the final game in both 1936 and 1937.

Gomez was at his best in 1937 against the Giants, beating them twice with complete games, 8-1 and 4-2. In the final game of the Series, he drove home the winning run with a single, a rousing achievement given that he was one of the worst hitters of the era.

Gomez went 6-0 with a 2.86 ERA in Series play. His record is the best ever among pitchers who went undefeated. The secret to his success? "Clean living and a fast outfield," the good-humored man would always say.

Lefty Gomez got a lift from Tony Lazzeri and Joe DiMaggio after holding the Giants to one run and six hits in Game 1.

SANDY

KOUFAX

1963 | LOS ANGELES DODGERS

Sandy Koufax once had this to say about baseball: "The game has a cleanness. If you do a good job, the numbers say so. You don't have to ask anyone, or play politics. You don't have to wait for the reviews." He should know. Nobody ever did a better job of pitching over a five-year period than Koufax did for the Los Angeles Dodgers starting in 1962. After years of inconsistent work, he was suddenly able to do anything he wanted with his hopping fastball and snapping curve. Instead of tensing up, which had been his bane, he took a deep breath, relaxed and reduced even the best hitters into so many Ray Oylers.

In the period from 1962 through 1966, Koufax had a 111-34 record and a 2.02 ERA. His ERA was the lowest in the National League for each of those years. Batters hit .197, .189, .191, .179 and .205 against him. He struck out more than 300 in three of those seasons, including 382 in 1965, which was the major league record until Nolan Ryan came along. He pitched a no-hitter in each of four consecutive seasons, the last a perfect game in 1965. He won the Cy Young Award three times in an era when only one was given for the major leagues, not one for each league.

Not that Koufax needed the help, but a rules change in 1963 made the strike zone bigger. He had perhaps his most dominating season, going 25-5 with 11 shutouts, a 1.88 ERA and 306 strikeouts in 311 innings. The Dodgers won the pennant, and it was like old times in the World Series, where they met the New York Yankees, their nemesis in so many Octobers

past when the two teams lived a subway ride away from each other. But those Brooklyn Dodgers had never had a pitcher the likes of Koufax, even though he had been on some of those teams. He beat Whitey Ford twice in five days as the Dodgers swept the 1963 Series in four games.

Koufax struck out the side in the first inning of Game 1. By the end of the day, he had struck out every Yankees regular except Clete Boyer. With his final pitch, he notched his 15th strikeout, breaking a 10-year-old Series record. The only damage against Koufax in his 5-2 victory was Tom Tresh's two-run home run in the eighth inning. After Johnny Podres beat the Yankees 4-1, and Don Drysdale pitched a 1-0 shutout, it was Koufax versus Ford again. Ford was marvelous, giving up only two hits, although one was a 450-foot home run by huge Frank Howard. Koufax gave up a home run to Mickey Mantle that tied the score. The Dodgers scored a run in the bottom of the seventh inning without the benefit of a hit, and Koufax completed the 2-1 victory. For his two games, he gave up 12 hits and three runs, walked three and struck out 23 in 18 innings. Two years later, he was on the mound again when the Dodgers won the Series, shutting out the Minnesota Twins 2-0 in Game 7.

This stupendous success might have gone on long past 1966, except that Koufax had developed an arthritic condition in his left elbow that caused him tremendous pain whenever he pitched. He won 27 games in 1966, then walked away from the game, done at age 30.

Sandy Koufax fired a strike in the first inning of Game 1. He struck out the first five Yankees, and his 15 K's for the game broke a 10-year-old Series record.

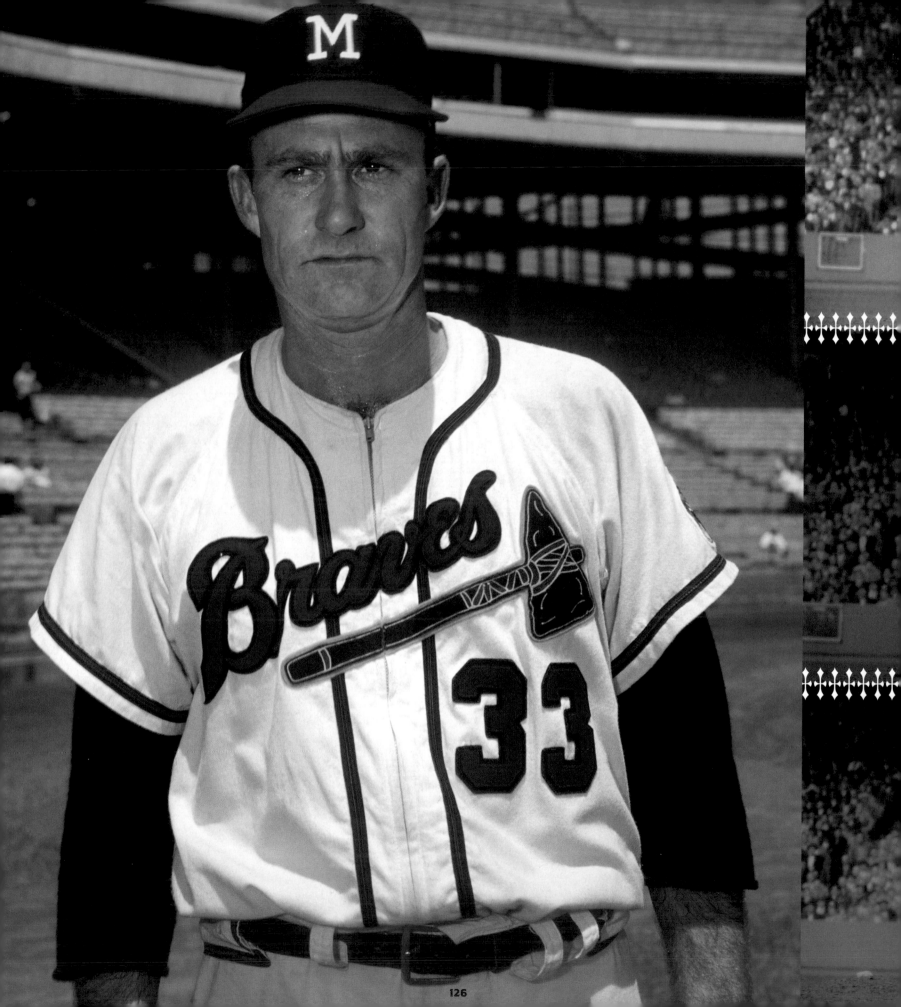

LEW BURDETTE

1957 | MILWAUKEE BRAVES

Few, if any, municipalities have ever embraced a sports team as warmly as Milwaukee did the Braves, who had lost all hope in Boston and packed up and moved to Suds City in the spring of 1953. "It wasn't just the Milwaukee people that made the Braves — it was the whole state of Wisconsin," said Johnny Logan, the team's shortstop in those years. "They were half drunk, but they all wanted to see the Braves. Oh, did they love us."

Baseball, beer and bratwurst were a winning combination for 13 seasons. Hank Aaron, Warren Spahn and Eddie Mathews were revered, but none of them warm the cold nights of Milwaukee Braves nostalgia quite like Lew Burdette. For it was Burdette who beat the mighty New York Yankees three times in 1957 and brought Milwaukee its one and only World Series championship.

Spahn was the ace of those teams and would end his career with more victories than any other lefthander in history, including 234 for the Milwaukee Braves. But as second bananas go, Burdette was one of the best, certainly the best to ever come out of Nitro, West Virginia, a town of some 20,000 that was born during World War I to produce the explosive powder nitrocellulose. Burdette, who won 173 times for the Milwaukee Braves, didn't throw hard, but he had uncanny control of his pitches and usually placed them low in the strike zone. He was suspected of throwing a spitball, a pitch that had been outlawed years earlier, but never got caught doing it.

The Braves of 1957 were young, bold and talented, but the Yankees were well seasoned and Series-tested, back for the ninth time in 11 years. Spahn lost Game 1. Burdette gave up two runs in the first three innings of Game 2, but the Yankees never touched him again. He completed that 4-2 victory, beat Whitey Ford 1-0 in Game 5 and then came back three days later for Game 7 and pitched a 5-0 shutout. In his 27 innings, Burdette walked only four (one intentionally) and struck out 13.

The Braves certainly needed superb pitching, given that they batted only .209 during the Series. Burdette was the first in 37 years to win three complete games in a Series and the first with two shutouts since Christy Mathewson had pitched three in 1905. Wisconsin will still drink to that.

Lew Burdette licked his fingers — some swear that he threw spitballs — and then delivered a pitch in his Game 7 shutout and third victory of the Series.

WHITEY FORD

1961 | NEW YORK YANKEES

The greatest pitcher in the history of the New York Yankees was a hometown boy. Whitey Ford was born in Manhattan and grew up in Queens. At 5-foot-10 and 180 pounds, he didn't look like much on a pitcher's mound and didn't throw particularly hard. But he had the guile of a burglar and the precision of a surgeon. He mixed fastballs, curveballs and changeups, controlled the strike zone, and stayed one mental click ahead of exasperated hitters. His pickoff move to first base was one of the best, and he was a superb fielder. Teammates called him "Slick" and said that his shoulders seemed to be broader than usual in tightly contested games. "Stick a baseball in his hand, and he became the most arrogant guy in the world," said Mickey Mantle, Ford's best friend.

CAREER LEADERS
VICTORIES

	W	L	WS	G
WHITEY FORD	10	8	11	22
BOB GIBSON	7	2	3	9
ALLIE REYNOLDS	7	2	6	15
RED RUFFING	7	2	7	10
LEFTY GOMEZ	6	0	5	7
CHIEF BENDER	6	4	5	10
WAITE HOYT	6	4	7	12

Ford was so good at his work that he won 69 percent of his decisions, the best rate of the 20th century among those who pitched at least 2,000 innings. He went 236-106 in his 16 seasons and likely would have won more except that his manager for the first nine years, Casey Stengel, let him pitch only every five days, instead of every four as was customary in the 1950s. Stengel was fearful of overusing Ford and risking injury to his star pitcher. That probably cost the Yankees the 1960 World Series and Stengel his job.

The pitcher who starts Game 1 can come back for Game 4 and again for Game 7. But in 1960 against the Pittsburgh Pirates, Stengel led off with Art Ditmar, who gave up three runs and didn't get out of the first inning. Ford started Game 3 and Game 6, and each time he pitched a shutout. But there was a Game 7. The pitchers on both sides got knocked around all afternoon until Bill Mazeroski, leading off the bottom of the ninth inning, hit his famous home run and won it for the Pirates, 10-9.

A few days later, the Yankees fired Stengel and replaced him with Ralph Houk, who did believe in a four-man pitching rotation. Ford achieved his best season ever in 1961. In that year's World Series, he pitched one shutout against the Cincinnati Reds and worked five innings of another shutout. He now had pitched 32 consecutive scoreless innings in the Series, which broke Babe Ruth's record of 29²/₃ set in 1916.

The San Francisco Giants finally scored against Ford in the second inning of Game 1 of the 1962 Series, ending his streak at 33²/₃ innings, which many consider to be the greatest pitching feat in Series history, given the duration and the competition. Ford had plenty of opportunity in the Series, appearing in 11 of them, and rarely faltered. His 10 victories, 94 strikeouts and 146 innings pitched are all records.

★★★★★★★★★★★★★★★★★★

1906–1910
CHICAGO CUBS

1996–2001
NEW YORK YANKEES

1910–1914
PHILADELPHIA ATHLETICS

1975–1996
CINCINNATI REDS

1915–1918
BOSTON RED SOX

1972–1974
OAKLAND ATHLETICS

1926–1928
NEW YORK YANKEES

1969–1971
BALTIMORE ORIOLES

1929–1931
PHILADELPHIA ATHLETICS

1947–1964
NEW YORK YANKEES

1936–1943
NEW YORK YANKEES

1942–1946
ST. LOUIS CARDINALS

★★★★★★★★★★★★★★★★★★

AN AMERICAN CLASSIC

SERIES
DYNASTIES

THE WORLD SERIES AT 100

CUBS

1906 TO 1910

Achievement

The Cubs won 69 percent of their games from 1906 to 1910 — the best five-year success rate of the 20th century — and went to four World Series. They beat the Detroit Tigers in both 1907 and 1908 without losing a game, although one of the five games in 1907 ended in a tie. The two world championships took the sting out of the 1906 Series for the Cubs, who had set a National League record by winning 116 games, but then lost in six games to their crosstown rivals, the White Sox, who were so lightly regarded that fans referred to them as the "Hitless Wonders." The Cubs won 104 games in 1909, but finished in second place. Connie Mack's mighty Philadelphia Athletics beat the Cubs in the 1910 Series.

Chance was safe at the plate during a 1910 game.

A winning combination: second baseman Johnny Evers, first baseman Frank Chance and shortstop Joe Tinker.

Cast

Frank Chance was just 27 when he became the Cubs manager during the 1905 season, but he quickly came to be so respected that he was called the "Peerless Leader." He also was the first baseman in the famed Tinker-to-Evers-to-Chance double play combination, and the most consistent hitter on those teams. The Cubs fielded virtually the same lineup throughout the five-year period. Johnny Kling, the team's highly regarded catcher, didn't play in 1909 because of a contract dispute.

Rise

It was the dead ball era, and the Cubs had what it took to win: speed, defense and pitching. Their guys stole 25 or more bases 19 times during the five-year period. The pitching staff's ERA was 1.76 or less in three of those years. Mordecai "Three Finger" Brown won 127 games and his ERAs ranged from 1.04 to 1.80. The Cubs won 92 games in 1905, but finished third. Prior to the 1906 season, they traded for third baseman Harry Steinfeldt, who proved to be the hitter and run producer they had lacked. He batted .327 in 1906 and led the league in RBIs with 83.

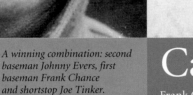

Peerless Leader

69%
WINNING PERCENTAGE FROM 1906–1910

Fall

Chance left after the 1912 season, and the Cubs slipped to fewer than 90 victories for the first time in 10 years. They made it back to the Series six more times during the next three decades but lost each time. For the last 55 years of the 20th century, they never finished better than second.

NEW YORK
YANKEES

4

WORLD CHAMPIONSHIPS
IN FIVE YEARS

It was four straight world championships for Derek Jeter and the Yankees after they beat the Mets in 2000.

Achievement

The Yankees went to five World Series in this six-year period and won four of them. They lost the first two games in 1996 to the Atlanta Braves, 12-1 and 4-0 in Yankee Stadium, then won the next four. In 1998, 1999 and 2000, the Yankees swept the San Diego Padres and the Braves, and beat the New York Mets in five games. The run ended in 2001 with a Game 7 loss to the Arizona Diamondbacks that was decided in the bottom of the ninth inning. Prior to the 2001 Series, the Yankees had a 53-18 record in postseason play since 1996 and had prevailed in 14 of 15 matchups.

Cast

Scott Brosius, Mariano Rivera and Jorge Posada after the decisive Game 4 in 1999.

The Yankees had not been to the World Series in 14 years and had not had a 90-win season in nine years, but their fortunes soared once Joe Torre became the manager in 1996. First baseman Tino Martinez, shortstop Derek Jeter, right fielder Paul O'Neill and center fielder Bernie Williams were regulars throughout the six-year period, and third baseman Scott Brosius and catcher Jorge Posada for the last four years. Andy Pettitte was in the pitching rotation for all six years, and Roger Clemens arrived in 1999. Mariano Rivera was the closer for five years. The wealthy Yankees did not buy this collection of champions. All but Clemens were either products of the team's farm system or acquired in trades.

Rise

Unlike previous Yankees dynasties, this one had no superstars that towered over the game. Rather, the Yankees of this period were highly efficient ballplayers who amounted to greatness as a group, rather than as individuals. The only big power season by an individual was Martinez's 44 homers and 141 RBIs in 1997. Martinez, Williams and O'Neill each producing an annual yield of 22 home runs and 107 RBIs was the norm. Jeter's batting average ranged from .291 to .349. The great 1998 team, which set an American League record with 114 victories, did not have a 30-homer man or a 125-RBI man, but four regulars were

Chad Curtis rode on his teammates' shoulders after he hit a home run in the 10th inning that ended Game 3 in 1999.

.300 hitters. Only three times in the six years did a pitcher achieve 20 victories — Pettitte, Clemens and David Cone — but 11 different pitchers won at least 10 games a total of 24 times. When a lead needed to be protected late in a game, Rivera did it 210 times from 1997 through 2001.

Fall

Brosius and O'Neill retired after the 2001 season, and Martinez wasn't re-signed. Still, the Yankees had a better record in 2002 than they had in all but one of the previous six seasons and won the American League East by a 10 1/2-game margin. But the pitching collapsed in the Division Series, surrendering 31 runs and 56 hits to the Anaheim Angels, who eliminated the Yankees in four games.

Coach Don Zimmer wore protection during the parade on Broadway for the 1999 champions.

PAUL O'NEILL

PHILADELPHIA
ATHLETICS

1910 TO 1914

HOME RUN BAKER

3
WORLD CHAMPIONSHIPS
IN FIVE YEARS

Achievement

The Athletics went to four World Series in this five-year period and won three of them. The 1910 and 1911 A's, considered the first great teams in the American League, beat the Chicago Cubs and the New York Giants in the Series. The 1913 squad again beat the Giants, but Boston's "Miracle Braves" swept the A's in 1914. The two world championships at the Giants' expense were sweet satisfaction for Connie Mack, whose early-1900s effort to launch a team in Philadelphia had been roundly hooted by Giants manager John McGraw. He called the franchise a "white elephant," a symbol the A's took to heart and still use as their logo.

CHIEF BENDER

EDDIE PLANK

Cast

Mack, who owned and managed the A's for 50 years, believed that pitchers accounted for 75 percent of a team's success, and by 1910 he had a staff full of good ones, including Eddie Plank and Chief Bender, who would make the Hall of Fame, and Jack Coombs, who probably would have, too, had illness not cut his career short. The pitchers benefited from Mack's famed $100,000 infield of Stuffy McInnis, Eddie Collins, Jack Barry and Home Run Baker. Collins was one of the great second basemen in history, and Baker was the American League's best power hitter of the dead ball era, leading in home runs four successive years starting in 1911.

Rise

The Detroit Tigers, featuring Ty Cobb, challenged the A's for a while in 1910 and 1911, but they didn't have the pitching to keep up. The 1913 and 1914 pennant races were closer, but the A's still had the best players.

Fall

All of the A's regulars were still in their prime in 1914. Plank and Coombs were on the way out, but Mack brought three promising young pitchers — Bob Shawkey, Bullet Joe Bush and Herb Pennock — to the team that year. The upstart Federal League, however, was coming after the major leagues' best players with big-money offers, a ploy that threatened to drive up everyone's payroll. Once Plank and Bender jumped, Mack determined he would not be able to afford all his stars, so he sold most of them and started over. By 1916 every player that mattered, except for McInnis and Bush, was gone. The A's fell into last place in 1915 and remained there for seven years, but the owner never once considered firing the manager.

CINCINNATI REDS

Achievement

In 1975, the Reds beat the Boston Red Sox in seven games in one of the most memorable Series ever. A year later, the Reds swept through postseason play with a 7-0 record, outscoring the Philadelphia Phillies and the New York Yankees 41-19. For the two years, Cincinnati was 14-3 in postseason play.

14-3
POSTSEASON RECORD

The main cogs lined up before Game 4 in 1976: manager Sparky Anderson, Pete Rose, Ken Griffey, Joe Morgan, Tony Perez, Dan Driessen, George Foster, Johnny Bench, Cesar Geronimo and Davey Concepcion.

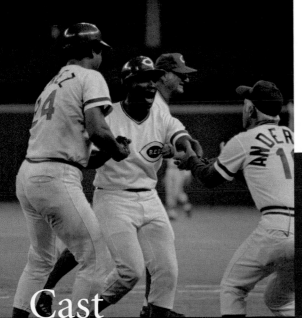

Perez and Sparky Anderson congratulated Joe Morgan after his game-winning hit in the 10th inning of Game 5 in 1975.

Johnny Bench waited for Tony Perez at home plate after Perez's three-run home run in Game 5 in 1975.

Cast

The Big Red Machine got wheels in 1970. A 35-year-old nobody named George "Sparky" Anderson became the manager that year, and Davey Concepcion joined Tony Perez, Pete Rose and Johnny Bench in the lineup. George Foster arrived a year later, and Joe Morgan and Cesar Geronimo in 1972. Ken Griffey, Sr. made the lineup during the 1974 season. Bench, Rose, Perez, Concepcion and Griffey, as well as Don Gullett and Gary Nolan, the top starting pitchers, were homegrown players. Morgan and Geronimo came in the same trade with Houston.

Rise

In the seven seasons from 1970 to 1976, the Reds averaged 98 victories a year, and won five division titles and National League pennants in 1970, 1972, 1975 and 1976. In the final two years of that era, they had a 69-19 record with the following lineup on the field: Perez at first base, Morgan at second, Concepcion as shortstop, Rose at third, Foster in left field, Geronimo in center, Griffey in right and Bench catching. All but Geronimo made the All-Star team in 1976. The 1975 and 1976 teams outscored their opponents by 192 runs. Bench, Concepcion, Morgan and Geronimo — the core of the defense — each won the Gold Glove at his position for four successive seasons starting in 1974.

JOE MORGAN

Fall

The Machine's alignment was knocked out of place when the highly respected Perez was traded after the 1976 season to make room for a promising kid, Dan Driessen. The team was never quite the same after that. The Los Angeles Dodgers, with better pitching than the Reds, moved to the top of the division. By the early 1980s, most of the Reds stars had taken advantage of free agency for higher-paying jobs elsewhere.

Perez and Bench celebrated the 1975 world championship.

BOSTON
RED SOX

Achievement

The Red Sox went to three World Series in this four-year period and won all of them. They beat both Philadelphia and Brooklyn in five games, and the Chicago Cubs in six games. The Red Sox had won five of the first 15 Series, but the rest of the 20th century passed without them hoisting another world championship trophy.

Harry Hooper batted first for the Red Sox in the bottom of the first inning of Game 1. He batted .333 in the Series.

Cast

The resourceful Red Sox lost two of their best players after the 1915 season but continued to win. Legendary center fielder Tris Speaker refused a pay cut and was traded, and his best friend, pitcher Smokey Joe Wood, sat out the season in protest. The Sox played most of the 1918 season with only outfielder Harry Hooper and shortstop Everett Scott left from their everyday

lineup of 1917; the rest had marched off to World War I. With a shortage of players, manager Ed Barrow decided to use Babe Ruth, one of his fine young pitchers, in the outfield or at first base on the days he didn't pitch. The Sox got six useful players during the four-year period from Connie Mack, who had undertaken a youth movement in Philadelphia and was unloading his veterans.

Rise

The Red Sox had assembled a formidable pitching staff by 1915, and Mack was breaking up the Athletics, who had won four of the previous five American League pennants. Wood, Ruth, Rube Foster, Dutch Leonard and Ernie Shore were superb, and when Wood was traded, the young Carl Mays was ready to take his place. When Speaker left, the Sox had to depend on left fielder Duffy Lewis and third baseman Larry Gardner for offense, until Ruth started taking regular cuts in 1918.

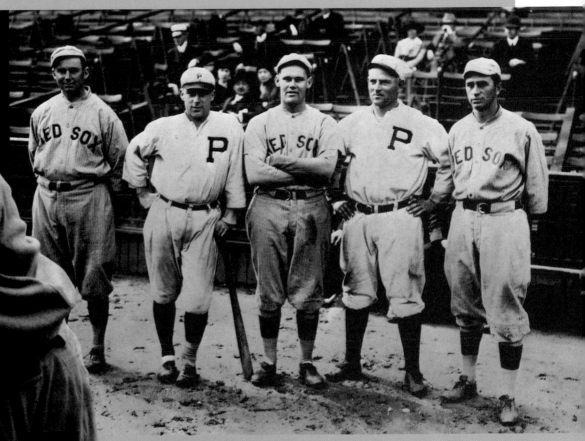

BABE RUTH

The Red Sox beat the Phillies in the 1915 World Series. Some of the players: Duffy Lewis, Ed Burns, Dutch Leonard, Gavvy Cravath and Harry Hooper.

Fall

The Red Sox never won the pennant by more than $2\frac{1}{2}$ games during the four-year period. When they slipped to sixth place in 1919, team owner Harry Frazee lost interest and began selling off players, including Ruth to the Yankees. It would be more than a decade before the Red Sox again ended a season with a winning

OAKLAND
ATHLETICS

REGGIE JACKSON

Achievement

The Athletics didn't win more than 94 games in any of the three seasons and twice needed all five games to win the League Championship Series. But they won all three World Series, beating the Cincinnati Reds (there were six one-run games), the New York Mets and the Los Angeles Dodgers. The first two Series went seven games, and the Dodgers fell in five.

142

Cast

A's owner Charles O. Finley was miserly, mean and stubborn. He probably never would have had a good team, except that starting in 1965, players no longer could choose who they would play for at the start of their career. The amateur free agent draft was instituted that year, and Finley's scouting minions more than proved their worth. The A's landed Rick Monday, Reggie Jackson, Sal Bando, Joe Rudi, Gene Tenace, Vida Blue and Rollie Fingers in the early drafts. Catfish Hunter, considered damaged goods by most clubs, and Blue Moon Odom, had signed in 1964, and before that Finley's scouts had found Bert Campaneris in Cuba. Monday eventually was sent to the Chicago Cubs in a trade that landed Ken Holtzman, and Finley later went back to the Cubs for Bill North. A championship nucleus was in place.

CATFISH HUNTER

Eight A's players, plus manager Alvin Dark and pitching coach Wes Stock, went to the 1975 All-Star Game. TOP ROW: Paul Lindblad, Rollie Fingers, Dark, Stock, Claudell Washington. BOTTOM ROW: Joe Rudi, Bert Campaneris, Gene Tenace, Reggie Jackson. Vida Blue missed the photo session.

Manager Alvin Dark and Reggie Jackson during the 1974 celebration.

Rise

The A's actually had their best season in 1971, the year that Dick Williams joined the team as manager. They won 101 games but were swept by Baltimore in the playoffs. For the next three years, the A's outscored their opponents by an average of more than one run per game. They won the American League West by only six, five and seven games — but they had a resolve to win whenever they had to win. North (107 stolen bases in two seasons) and Campaneris (120 steals in three seasons) got on base, and Jackson (86 home runs, 278 RBIs), Bando (66, 278) and Rudi (59, 240) paid the bills. Hunter won 67 games, Holtzman 59 and Blue 43. Fingers had 61 saves. They united against a common cause — Finley — and won for themselves, although they did not always get along, as evidenced by a few clubhouse altercations along the way.

3 WORLD CHAMPIONSHIPS IN THREE YEARS

Fall

Williams, disgusted with Finley, left after the 1973 season, but Alvin Dark proved to be a capable replacement. The end really began when Hunter, taking advantage of a contract breach by Finley, left for the New York Yankees after the 1974 season. Finley didn't have the money or the inclination to pay the market rate for his stars, and all were gone by 1977. Instead of Bando, the third baseman was Wayne Gross. Instead of Jackson and Rudi in the outfield, it was Mitchell Page and Jim Tyrone. Instead of Fingers, it was Bob "Spacey" Lacey. The A's finished last in 1977, behind the expansion Seattle Mariners, and they didn't fully recover until the late 1980s, revitalized by new ownership.

YANKEES

Achievement

The Yankees went to the World Series in each of the three years. They lost Game 7 to the St. Louis Cardinals in 1926, stopped in the late innings by the relief heroics of old Pete Alexander. The 1927 team, which won 110 games, the most in American League history until 1954, and the 1928 team both swept the Series. They beat the Pittsburgh Pirates and the Cardinals by a combined score of 50-20.

A championship infield: first baseman Lou Gehrig, second baseman Tony Lazzeri, shortstop Mark Koenig and third baseman Joe Dugan.

MARK KOENIG

Cast

Miller Huggins was the manager, and the lineup was the same throughout the three-year period, except at catcher, where there really wasn't a regular. Pat Collins and Johnny Grabowski shared the position, but both looked over their shoulders and waited for the young Bill Dickey to punch their tickets back to Palookaville. The great outfielders — Bob Meusel in left, Earle Combs in center and Babe Ruth in right — all were in their prime years. Lou Gehrig had replaced Wally Pipp in 1925, and second baseman Tony Lazzeri was a heralded rookie in 1926. The pitching staff started with Herb Pennock and Waite Hoyt, one of the great lefty/righty combinations in history. How good were the main players in this cast? Ruth, Gehrig, Combs, Lazzeri, Pennock and Hoyt, plus Huggins and general manager Ed Barrow all are in the Hall of Fame.

Rise

The Yankees finished seventh in 1925, their worst showing in 12 years. Ruth was stricken with his famous "bellyache" that kept him out until June. Heads might have rolled had Gehrig, Combs and shortstop Mark Koenig not earned jobs and shown promise that portended better days ahead. During the next three years, the Yankees outscored their opponents by an incredible 719 runs, an average of 1.6 per game. The 1927 and the 1928 teams each had five .300 hitters playing every day. Ruth bashed 161 home runs and Gehrig 90, and together they accounted for almost 900 RBIs. Hoyt won 61 games, and Pennock 59. Wilcey Moore leaped from a Class B league to the Yankees in 1927 and, pitching whenever he was needed, won 19 games and saved 13. In 1928, hard-throwing but wild George Pipgras had the season of his life, winning 24 games.

Fall

Falling is a relative term when it concerns the Yankees. From 1929 to 1935, they never fell further than third place, and that happened only once. But they also won one pennant, in 1932, when they swept the Cubs in a Series in which Ruth, the legend goes, called his shot. A new era dawned for the Yankees in 1936, and it was a dandy.

MILLER HUGGINS

HERB PENNOCK

1969 TO 1971

Achievement

The Orioles went to three successive World Series. The 1969 team, whose 109 victories was the most in the major leagues since 1954, lost in five games to New York's "Miracle Mets." The 1970 Orioles, considered one of the best teams ever, beat the Cincinnati Reds in five games. The 1971 team lost to the Pittsburgh Pirates in seven games.

JIM PALMER

DAVE MCNALLY

MIKE CUELLAR

EARL WEAVER

Cast

DON BUFORD

The Orioles' juggernaut first took form in 1966, the year that Frank Robinson joined the team. Most of the other key members — third baseman Brooks Robinson, first baseman Boog Powell, second baseman Davey Johnson, center fielder Paul Blair and pitchers Dave McNally and Jim Palmer — were in place. The Orioles won the pennant and then pitched three shutouts and swept the Los Angeles Dodgers in the World Series. The team slipped the next two seasons, mainly because Palmer and Wally Bunker, another exceptional young pitcher, endured serious arm problems. Earl Weaver took over as manager midway through the 1968 season, and a year later the Orioles began to soar.

20-GAME WINNERS IN THREE YEARS

DAVEY JOHNSON

BROOKS ROBINSON

Rise

The Orioles won 318 games during the three-year period, finished in first place by a combined 46 games, and were 9-0 in three League Championship Series. They pitched and played defense better than any other team, and they had a well-balanced lineup. Johnson, Brooks Robinson, Blair and shortstop Mark Belanger were perennial Gold Glove winners. Don Buford was a clever leadoff hitter, and Boog Powell and the Robinson boys provided power. Palmer came back healthy in 1969, and the pitching staff had nine 20-game winners during the three years, including four in 1971, only the second time that had happened since 1920.

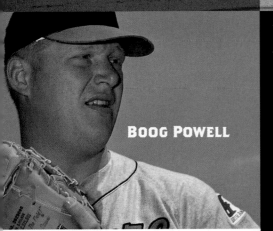

BOOG POWELL

FRANK ROBINSON

Fall

The Orioles didn't fall far. After 1971, they won at least 90 games in five of the next seven seasons, but had only two division titles to show for it. First, the Oakland Athletics dominated the league, and then the New York Yankees. Both Frank and Brooks Robinson were done as superstars after 1971. Frank finished his career with other teams; Brooks stayed and didn't help much with his bat, but he continued to play the best defense in history at third base.

LEFT: *Four 20-game winners in 1971: Palmer, McNally, Pat Dobson and Cuellar.*

PHILADELPHIA
ATHLETICS

Achievement

The Athletics went to three World Series in this three-year period and won the first two. They beat the Chicago Cubs in five games and the St. Louis Cardinals in six. The 1931 team that went 107-45, the best record of the 1930s, lost to the Cardinals in seven games, undone by the heroics of Pepper Martin. The A's three-year record of 313-143 is the third best all-time.

313-143
A's RECORD FROM 1929–1931

GEORGE EARNSHAW

LEFTY GROVE

79-15

PITCHING RECORD FROM 1929–1931

Cast

In 1925, 11 years after the big-talking Federal League scared Connie Mack into selling off his championship team, the Athletics owner and manager again was fielding a respectable team, and it soon became a championship team. Ironically, the A's were built around players that Mack purchased. He got two great pitchers, Lefty Grove and George Earnshaw, plus two regulars from Baltimore's minor league team. Mack also bought the Portland, Oregon, minor league franchise to get catcher Mickey Cochrane; grabbed outfielder Al Simmons from the Milwaukee minor league team and signed a 16-year-old high school dropout who grew up to be the great first baseman Jimmie Foxx. Mack, Grove, Cochrane, Simmons and Foxx are all in the Hall of Fame.

Rise

The A's scored 718 runs more than their opponents did during the three-year period. Foxx, in his early 20s, averaged 33 home runs, 131 RBIs and .327. Simmons, in his late 20s, averaged 31 home runs, 149 RBIs and .378. Cochrane wasn't a power hitter, but he was nevertheless a superb hitter, averaging .345, 11 home runs and 90 RBIs. Grove had a spectacular 79-15 record during the period. Earnshaw won 65 games and Rube Walberg 51.

Fall

The A's won 94 games in 1932, but finished a distant second to the New York Yankees. The Great Depression was setting in and Mack was concerned about his payroll, which he claimed was the highest in the major leagues. After the 1932 season, he sold Simmons and two others to the Chicago White Sox, and by 1934 all the stars were gone. It would be 40 years and two franchise shifts before the A's again were great.

NEW YORK
YANKEES

Achievement

The Yankees went to 15 World Series in this 18-year period and won 10 of them. They beat six different teams, including the Brooklyn Dodgers five times. They won Game 7 five times and lost it four times. They were 52-41 for the period. They slipped at the end, losing in both 1963 and 1964.

Hank Bauer, Joe DiMaggio and Gene Woodling headed for the visitors clubhouse at the Polo Grounds after the Yankees won Game 4 in 1951.

Cast

The Yankees had three managers during the period, and each won in the Series, but most of the success came under Casey Stengel, who was in charge from 1949 to 1960. The roster went through several generations. The early

Rise

The Yankees never strayed far from first place because they usually had the best of everything. During this 18-year period, here's how they ranked in the American League in four categories: runs scored: first or second, 17 times; home runs: first, second or third, 16 times; batting average: first, second or third, 15 times; earned run average: first, second or third, 18 times. The stars shone brightest. The Yankees had 16 30-homer seasons, all by DiMaggio, Mantle, Berra and Maris. Their 15 100-RBI seasons also belonged to those four, plus one for Joe Pepitone. There were eight different 20-game winners, with only Vic Raschi and Whitey Ford reaching that level more than once.

WORLD SERIES APPEARANCES IN 18 YEARS

1949 celebrators: Yogi Berra, Gene Woodling, Phil Rizzuto, manager Casey Stengel, Cliff Mapes (behind Stengel), Gus Niarhos and Joe Page (foreground).

Yogi Berra caught Pee Wee Reese's pop-up in Game 6 in 1956.

Fall

Howard, Mantle and Maris all suffered injuries in 1965 that took them out of the lineup for extended periods. Ford was 36, and Jim Bouton, who had won 39 games the previous two seasons, went 4-15. The Yankees tumbled to sixth place, 25 games out of first. And it would get worse. They fell to last place in 1966, and weren't taken seriously again until 1974. The amateur free agent draft that was instituted in 1965 restricted the Yankees' ability to outbid everyone else for the best prospects and prolonged their rebuilding process.

MICKEY MANTLE

stars were Joe DiMaggio, Phil Rizzuto, Tommy Henrich and Allie Reynolds. Yogi Berra first showed up in 1947, and was joined by Whitey Ford and Mickey Mantle a few years later. DiMaggio passed the legend

torch to Mantle in 1951. Management always made sure the supporting cast was worthy of the stars. Hank Bauer and Enos Slaughter were near the end, but still helpful. Elston Howard came from the Negro Leagues.

Roger Maris, Clete Boyer and Art Ditmar were swiped from unsuspecting Kansas City. Ralph Terry was sent to Kansas City and then brought back. Bob Turley came from Baltimore, and Tony Kubek

and Bobby Richardson came from the farm system. There was always a good kid in the system to trade for someone who could help right now.

Joe DiMaggio, surrounded by teammates, during the 1950 World Series.

NEW YORK
YANKEES

BILL DICKEY

JOE DiMAGGIO

CHARLIE KELLER

GEORGE SELKIRK

1937 YANKEES

Achievement

The Yankees went to seven World Series in this eight-year period and won six of them. They beat five different teams — the New York Giants twice — and lost only to the St. Louis Cardinals. None of the Series went seven games. In the six world championship years, the Yankees had a 24-5 Series record and scored more than twice as many runs as their opponents. Many consider the 1939 Yankees, who went 106-45 and crushed the Cincinnati Reds in four games in the Series, to be the greatest team of all time.

152

Cast

Joe McCarthy was the manager for the entire run. The lineup was remarkably stable, except at first base, until the final year of the era, when Joe DiMaggio, Phil Rizzuto, Tommy Henrich and Red Ruffing went off to World War II. Lou Gehrig was all but finished by the end of the 1938 season, and four different guys manned first base for the next five years. Both the second base and shortstop positions passed from one superb player to another during the era, Tony Lazzeri giving way to Joe Gordon and Frankie

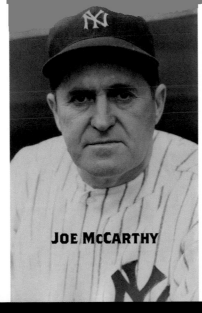

JOE McCARTHY

Crosetti to Rizzuto. Red Rolfe was the third baseman until the final year, and Bill Dickey was the catcher the entire time. DiMaggio was a rookie in 1936. He and three others — Henrich, George Selkirk and Charlie Keller — were the primary outfielders. The Yankees' great pitchers of the era were Ruffing, Lefty Gomez, Spud Chandler and Johnny Murphy. A lot of credit went to general manager Ed Barrow, who also was in charge during the Yankees' great run in the 1920s.

Rise

In their seven pennant-winning seasons from 1936 to 1943, the Yankees averaged 102 victories and finished in first place by an average of 14 games. They outscored their opponents by more than 1,900 runs, an average of 1.8 per game. DiMaggio averaged .339, 31 homers and 133 RBIs, and he had plenty of help. Gehrig was still a huge force in 1936 and 1937. Seven players accounted for 24 20–home run seasons and 22 100-RBIs seasons that the Yankees achieved during this eight-year period. Ruffing won 126 games and was a four-time 20-game winner. Gomez won 88, and Chandler won 78. Murphy, the best relief pitcher of the era, won 56 and saved 83.

SPUD CHANDLER

BILL DICKEY

1937 celebrators: (seated) Joe DiMaggio; (standing) manager Joe McCarthy, team owner Jacob Ruppert, Lou Gehrig and Tony Lazzeri.

Fall

DiMaggio, Rizzuto, Henrich and Ruffing didn't return from the war until 1946, and by that time Ruffing was 42. Losing those stars leveled the playing field, and the Yankees finished no better than third from 1944 through 1946. By 1947, the war guys were back on pace, fresh talent was bubbling up from the organization's farm clubs, and the Yankees were off on another dynastic run, this one to last into the 1960s.

Joe DiMaggio scored the winning run in the ninth inning of Game 4 in 1941, after Tommy Henrich (7) had scored the tying run. The catcher was Mickey Owen.

ST. LOUIS
CARDINALS

Achievement

The Cardinals went to four World Series in this five-year period and won three of them. In Game 1 of 1942, they made four errors, didn't get a hit until the eighth inning and lost 7-4, but they swept the next four games from the New York Yankees. The Cardinals lost to the Yankees in five games in 1943, but they beat the city-rival Browns in 1944 and the Boston Braves in 1946.

Whitey Kurowski, Enos Slaughter, Marty Marion and Stan Musial in 1946.

Walker Cooper (15) and Johnny Hopp (12) greeted Stan Musial after he scored in Game 4 of the 1944 World Series.

1946 celebrators: Enos Slaughter, Harry Brecheen, manager Eddie Dyer and Harry Walker.

1942 celebrators: (seated) manager Billy Southworth and Walker Cooper; (standing) Enos Slaughter, Stan Musial, Johnny Beazley and Whitey Kurowski.

Cast

The fabled "Gas House Gang" grew old in the mid-1930s, but the Cardinals were respectable again by 1939, largely because of club president Branch Rickey's far-flung minor league system. He had arrangements with more than 30 clubs, and from those came outfielders Stan Musial, Enos Slaughter and Terry Moore; shortstop Marty Marion; catcher Walker Cooper; and pitchers Mort Cooper, Walker's older brother, and Johnny Beazley. That was the core of the team, and even when Slaughter, Moore, and Beazley marched off to World War II in 1943, the Cardinals kept winning because they had more help from their farm system. St. Louis won 106, 105 and 105 games from 1942 to 1944.

4 IN 5 YEARS

Sportsman's Park, Game 5 of the 1943 World Series. The Yankees' Bill Dickey, running between second and third, had just hit a two-run home run.

Rise

The Cardinals came of age in the 1942 National League pennant race. They trailed the Brooklyn Dodgers by a wide margin in early August, but won 43 of their final 51 games and finished in first place by two games. Musial, a 21-year-old rookie, batted .315, the first of his 16 consecutive .300 seasons. He would become the greatest player in Cardinals history, but those teams of the early 1940s didn't have to rely on any one player. Mort Cooper was the league MVP in 1942, Musial in 1943 and Marion in 1944.

Max Lanier (center) got the hero's treatment after pitching three scoreless innings and gaining the victory in Game 4 in 1942.

Fall

Rickey, who long had a contentious relationship with the Cardinals ownership, resigned in a huff after the 1942 Series and went to the Dodgers. He left behind a fine team that would finish first or second every year until 1950. By that time, the only star left was Musial, and the farm system pipeline, no longer being primed by Rickey, had dried up.